The New Global Society

Globalization
and Poverty

The New Global Society

Globalization and Development
Globalization and Human Rights
Globalization and Labor
Globalization and Poverty
Globalization and the Physical Environment
Globalization, Language, and Culture

Globalization and Poverty

Nadejda Ballard

Foreword by
James Bacchus
Chairman, Global Trade Practice Group
of Greenberg Traurig, Professional Association

Introduction by
Ilan Alon, Ph.D.
Crummer Graduate School of Business
Rollins College

CHELSEA HOUSE
PUBLISHERS
A Haights Cross Communications Company ®
Philadelphia

COVER: Migrant farm workers spend the night on the sidewalk in downtown El Paso in July, 1997.

CHELSEA HOUSE PUBLISHERS
VP, NEW PRODUCT DEVELOPMENT Sally Cheney
DIRECTOR OF PRODUCTION Kim Shinners
CREATIVE MANAGER Takeshi Takahashi
MANUFACTURING MANAGER Diann Grasse

Staff for GLOBALIZATION AND POVERTY

EXECUTIVE EDITOR Lee Marcott
EDITORIAL ASSISTANT Carla Greenberg
PRODUCTION EDITOR Bonnie Cohen
PHOTO EDITOR Sarah Bloom
SERIES AND COVER DESIGNER Keith Trego
LAYOUT 21st Century Publishing and Communications, Inc.

©2006 by Chelsea House Publishers,
a subsidiary of Haights Cross Communications.
All rights reserved. Printed and bound in China.

A Haights Cross Communications ⟋ Company ®

www.chelseahouse.com

First Printing

9 8 7 6 5 4 3 2 1

Library of Congress Cataloging-in-Publication Data

Ballard, Nadejda
   Globalization and poverty/Nadejda Ballard.
      p. cm.—(The new global society)
   Includes bibliographical references and index.
   ISBN 0-7910-8188-5 (hard cover)
   1. Poverty. 2. Globalization. I. Title. II. Series.
HC79.P6B33 2005
362.5'09'0511—dc22
                                                            2005015047

Contents

Foreword

by James Bacchus

IT'S A SMALL WORLD AFTER ALL

One reason that I know this is true is because I have a daughter
who adores Walt Disney World in my hometown of Orlando,
Florida. When Jamey was small, she and I would go to
Walt Disney World together. We would stand together in a
long line waiting to ride her very favorite ride—"Small
World." We would stand together in those long lines over
and over again.

Jamey is in high school now, but, of course, she still adores
Walt Disney World, and she and I still stand together from
time to time in those same long lines—because she never tires
of seeing "Small World." She is not alone. Seemingly endless
lines of children have stood waiting for that same ride through
the years, hand in hand with their parents, waiting for the
chance to take the winding boat ride through Disney's "Small
World." When their chance has come, they have seen the vast
variety of the world in which we live unfold along the winding
way as it appears to the child in all of us. Hundreds of dancing
dolls adorn an array of diverse and exotic settings from around
the world. In the echoing voice of a song they sing together—
over and over again—they remind all those along for the ride
that ours is a world of laughter, a world of tears, a world of
hopes, and a world of fears.

And so it is. So it appears when we are children, and so it
surely appears when we put childhood behind us and try to

assume our new roles as "grown-ups" in what is supposed to be the adult world. The laughter, the tears, the hopes, the fears, are all still there in a world that, to our grown-up eyes, keeps getting smaller every day. And, even when we are no longer children, even when we are now grown-ups, we don't really know what to do about it.

The grown-up name for our small world is "globalization." Our globalizing world is getting smaller every day. Economically and otherwise, our world is becoming a place where we all seem to be taking the same ride. Advances in information, transportation, and many other technologies are making distance disappear, and are making next-door neighbors of all of us, whatever our nationality, whatever our costume, whatever the song we sing.

When Walt Disney first introduced the "Small World" ride at the World's Fair in New York in 1964, I was in high school, and we could still pretend that, although the world was getting smaller, it still consisted of many different places. But no more. The other day, I took a handheld device, called a "BlackBerry," out of my pocket and e-mailed instructions to a colleague in my law firm regarding a pending legal matter. I was on a train in the Bavarian mountains in Germany, while my colleague was thousands of miles away in the United States. In effect, we were in the same small place.

This is just one example of our ever-smaller world. And, however small it seems to me in my middle age, and however smaller it may become in my lifetime, it is likely to shrink all the more for my daughter Jamey and for every other young American attending high school today.

Hence, we announce this new series of books for high school students on some of the results of globalization. These results inspire hope, shown in the efforts of so many around the world to respond to the challenges posed by globalization by making international laws, building international institutions, and seeking new ways to live and work together in our smaller world. Those results also inspire fear, as evidenced by streets filled with anti-globalization protesters in Seattle, London, and other globalized cities around the world.

It is hard to tell truth from fiction in assessing the results of globalization. The six volumes in this series help us to do so. Does globalization promote worldwide economic development, or does it hinder it? Does it reduce poverty, or does it increase it? Does it enhance culture, or does it harm it? Does it advance the cause of human rights, or does it impede it? Does it serve the cause of workers' rights, or does it slow it? Does it help the environment, or does it hurt it? These are the important questions posed in these volumes. The hope is that in asking these questions the series will help young people find answers to them that will prove to be better than those found thus far by "grown-ups."

I have had the privilege of trying to begin the process of finding some of these answers. I have helped negotiate international trade agreements for the United States. I have served as a member of the Congress of the United States. I have been one of seven jurists worldwide on the court of final appeal that helps the 148 countries that are Members of the World Trade Organization to uphold international trade rules and to peacefully resolve international trade disputes. I am one of these who see far more reason for hope than for fear in the process of globalization.

I believe we will all be more likely to see globalization in this way if we recall the faces of the dancing dolls in Disney's "Small World." Those dolls are from many different countries. They wear many different costumes. But their faces are very much the same. The song they sing is the same. And, in that song, they remind us all that as we all ride together, "There's so much that we share, that it's time we're aware it's a small world, after all." Indeed it is. And, if we remember all that we in the world share—if we remember above all, our shared humanity—then we will be much more likely to make globalization a reason to hope that our smaller world will also be a better world.

James Bacchus
Chairman, Global Trade Practice Group
of Greenberg Traurig, Professional Association
April 2005

Introduction

by Ilan Alon

Globalization is now an omnipresent phenomenon in society, economics, and politics, affecting industry and government, and all other walks of life in one form or another. THE NEW GLOBAL SOCIETY series gives the reader a well-rounded understanding of the forces of globalization and its multifaceted impact on our world. The international flavor is evident in the make-up of the authors in the series, who include one Israeli, one New Zealander, one Bulgarian, one Korean, and two American scholars. In addition to an international slate of authors, many of whom have lived and worked around the world, the writers hail from fields as diverse as economics, business, comparative literature, and journalism. Their varied experiences and points of view bring a comprehensive and diverse analysis to the topics they write about.

While the books were written to stand alone, those readers who complete all six will find many points of commonality between the books and many instances where observations from one book can be directly applied to points made in another.

These books are written for the lay person and include definitions of key terms and ideas and many examples that help the reader make the ideas more concrete. The books are short and non-technical and are intended to spur the reader to read more about globalization outside these books and in other sources such as magazines, newspapers, journals, Internet sources, and other books on the topics. The discussion of the positive and negative aspects of the consequences of globalization, both here and abroad, will allow the reader to make their own judgments about the merits and demerits of globalization.

A brief description of each of the six books in the series follows:

Globalization and Development—Eugene D. Jaffe

Eugene D. Jaffe of the Graduate School of Business, Bar-Ilan University, Israel, and current Visiting Professor at Copenhagen Business School, Denmark, explains the key terms and concepts of globalization and its historical development. Specifically, it ties globalization to economic development and examines globalization's impact on both developed and developing countries. Arguments for and against globalization are presented. The relevance of globalization for the American economy is specifically addressed.

There are many illustrations of the concepts through stories and case examples, photographs, tables, and diagrams. After reading this book, students should have a good understanding of the positive and negative aspects of globalization and will be better able to understand the issues as they appear in the press and other media.

Globalization and Labor—Peter Enderwick

Peter Enderwick is Professor of International Business, Auckland University of Technology, New Zealand, and a long-time researcher on international labor issues. His book provides a discussion of the impact of globalization on labor with a focus on employment, earnings, staffing strategies, and human resource management within global business. Contemporary issues and concerns such as offshore sourcing, labor standards, decreasing social mobility, and income inequality are treated. The book contains many case examples and vignettes illustrating that while globalization creates both winners and losers, there are opportunities to increase the beneficial effects through appropriate policy.

Globalization and Poverty—Nadejda Ballard

Nadejda Ballard is a professional international business consultant with clients in the United States and Europe and is an adjunct instructor for international business at Rollins College, Winter Park, Florida. In addition to her extensive experience living and working in various countries, Nadejda is also a native of Bulgaria, a developing country that is struggling with many of the issues discussed in her book.

Globalization, which is reshaping our society at all levels from the individual to the national and regional, is also changing the way we define poverty and attempt to combat it. The book includes the ideas of academics and researchers as well as those who are charged at the practical level with grappling with the issues of world poverty. Unlike other books on the subject, her aim is not to promote a certain view or theory, but to provide a realistic overview of the current situation and the strategies intended to improve it. The book is rich with such visual aids as maps, photographs, tables, and charts.

Globalization and the Environment—Ho-Won Jeong

Howon Jeong teaches at the Institute for Conflict Analysis and Resolution at George Mason University and is author of *Global Environmental Policymaking*. His new book for Chelsea House discusses the major global impacts of human activities on the environment including global warming, ozone depletion, the loss of biological diversity, deforestation, and soil erosion, among other topics. This book explores the interrelationship of human life and nature. The earth has finite resources and our every action has consequences for the future. The effects of human consumption and pollution are felt in every corner of the globe. How we choose to live will affect generations to come. The book should generate an awareness of the ongoing degradation of our environment and it is hoped that this awareness will serve as a catalyst for action needed to be undertaken for and by future generations.

Globalization, Culture, and Language—Richard E. Lee
Richard E. Lee teaches world literature and critical theory at the College of Oneonta, State University of New York. The author believes that globalization is a complex phenomenon of contemporary life, but one with deep ties to the past movements of people and ideas around the world. By placing globalization within this historical context, the author casts the reader as part of those long-term cultural trends.

The author recognizes that his American audience is largely composed of people who speak one language. He introduces such readers to the issues related to a multilingual, global phenomenon. Readers will also learn from the book that the cultural impacts of globalization are not merely a one-way street from the United States to the rest of the world. The interconnectedness of the modern world means that the movements of ideas and people affect everyone.

Globalization and Human Rights—Alma Kadragic
Alma Kadragic is a journalist, a writer, and an adjunct professor at Phoenix University. She was a writer and producer for ABC News in New York, Washington D.C., and London for 16 years. From 1983–89 she was ABC News bureau chief in Warsaw, Poland, and led news coverage of the events that led to the fall of Communism in Poland, Hungary, Czechoslovakia, East Germany, and Yugoslavia.

Her book links two of the fundamental issues of our time: globalization and human rights. Human rights are the foundation on which the United States was established in the late

18th century. Today, guarantees of basic human rights are included in the constitutions of most countries.

The author examines the challenges and opportunities globalization presents for the development of human rights in many countries. Globalization often brings changes to the way people live. Sometimes these changes expand human rights, but sometimes they threaten them. Both the positive and negative impacts of globalization on personal freedom and other measures of human rights are examined. She also considers how the globalization of the mass media can work to protect the human rights of individuals in any country.

All of the books in THE NEW GLOBAL SOCIETY series examine both the pros and the cons of the consequences of globalization in an objective manner. Taken together they provide the readers with a concise and readable introduction to one of the most pervasive and fascinating phenomena of our time.

Dr. Ilan Alon, Ph.D
Crummer Graduate School of Business
Rollins College
April 2005

Poverty in the New Millennium

Bakyt: Missing Out on School and Play Because of Poverty

Bakyt is an 11-year-old boy living in southern Kyrgyzstan, in a town called Kokyangak. During the Soviet period, coal mining was the town's main industry, but it is now dying out. In Bakyt's family, the children are the main breadwinners: he and his two older brothers (the eldest is 16 years old) work in a coal mine. Bakyt's mother was disabled two years ago and cannot walk. She receives a monthly pension of about 450 Soms (approx. $10.35). Bakyt's father does not provide any support to the family. Bakyt's grandmother is old and sick. The family's two-bedroom house is run-down—the windows are broken and it is very cold in winter. They rarely heat the house because they cannot afford to buy wood. Bakyt's 13-year-old sister looks after their mother and grandmother, and often misses school for a month at a time because of her caring duties at home. One of Bakyt's older brothers is training to become a welder at a vocational college. His college tuition is free; however, he very often misses college because of his work. Bakyt's other brother does not attend school—he works in the fields in neighboring Uzgen in spring and summer and in the mine in autumn and winter.

Inside the mine where Bakyt and his brothers work, space is very tight and the tunnels are narrow, which is why it falls to children as young as 9 to carry out sacks full of coal—there isn't enough space for the adult miners to do this. The lack of support structures inside the mine means that there is a very real danger that the tunnels could collapse at any time.

When Bakyt is not working in the mine, he and his sister collect bricks from building demolition sites and sell them. They earn 1 Som per brick (approx. $0.23), as long as it is not broken or damaged. Bakyt says, "I am not afraid of work, what is more important is how much they pay me. In autumn and winter my brothers and I earn up to 200 Soms ($4.60) a day altogether. In the spring and summer, though, we earn 25–30 Soms ($0.575–0.69) a day and that is not even every day. Working inside a mine is dangerous, dusty, there is not enough air inside, but you get used to it. Our work begins at 7–8 in the morning, and we sometimes carry on till 6 in the evening. We take our lunch with us. Mostly we bring *airan* (plain yoghurt), bread, tea and potato for lunch."

Bakyt's family does not consume butter at all and drinks tea without sugar. They cannot afford to buy much tea, so they dry the tea bags and re-use them several times. Sometimes they gather mint for cooking foods like *pelmeni* (a pastry with mint filling, though it would be made with meat if they could afford it). Bakyt says: "My favorite food is soup with meat, but we have not made this for a long time. It is very expensive and my mother cannot afford it on her pension. If I made a lot of money, first of all I would buy meat and cook soup for my mother, grandma and sister."

Due to malnutrition and hard physical work, Bakyt and his sister are often ill, and last winter they both suffered from bronchitis. Bakyt is very concerned about his family's poor health: "Thoughts about my mother's disease and the fact that I cannot help her always bother me. Grandma is sick too, and cannot walk either. Anara and me, both of us are always coughing as soon as winter arrives. I always pray for everybody's health. Those who are poor, they should not get sick. If you are not healthy and do not have money nobody needs you. This is the case with our mother—nobody needs her except us. We do not have relatives who would help us if we fall sick."

Bakyt does well at school, but in order to earn money to buy food for the family, he often skips school and goes out to work instead. Although he does not have to pay school fees, attending school regularly is still difficult, partly because his family depends on the income he earns, and partly because he does not have money to buy books and other school materials. In winter, he often does not go to school because he cannot afford warm clothing suitable for the season, which he says is not uncommon: "There are many of us in my class who miss school very often because of clothes and work. I would like to study and study normally. I like to study and I know that if you are not educated you never get a good job. I have not decided yet what I am going to become, but I at least have to graduate high school and then I can somehow help my mother and the whole family. But I do not know how that is going to happen."

Talking about what he would like to see change in the future, Bakyt says: "I do not know what the future holds for me and my brothers; sometimes I am horrified thinking about it, but I hope for a better future. Every day before I go to sleep, I pray for my mother's and grandma's health. I ask God that my brothers find a better job, and for my sister Anara to attend school. I also pray for myself—I would like to go to school and graduate high school. I do not want to see my mother crying into her pillow, I do not want us to eat mint and I do not want us to have to think about what we will eat tomorrow."[1]

Source: "Bakyt: Missing Out on School and Play Because of Poverty," case study. Copyright Childhood Research and Policy Center. Reprinted with permission.

DEFINING POVERTY IN THE ERA OF GLOBALIZATION

We will spare no effort to free our fellow men, women and children from the abject and dehumanizing conditions of extreme poverty, to which more than a billion of them are currently subjected.

—UN Millennium Declaration[2]

In the early 1990s, the United Nations (UN) assembled a global agenda for solving the most urgent issues facing the world today and summarized it in the Millennium Declaration. Above is one of the statements in the Declaration, which was accepted at the Millennium Assembly of the United Nations[3] in September 2000.

Based on the statements in the declaration, the UN developed eight specific Millennium Development Goals (MDGs) to be accomplished by the years 2015 or 2020. The First Millennium Development Goal is to "Eradicate Extreme Poverty and Hunger." More specifically, it aims to decrease the number of people living on less than $1 a day to 14.2 percent of all people living outside the developed countries by 2015, or to half their 1990 level. Another goal is to reduce the number of people who suffer from hunger by 50 percent by 2015.[4]

Figure 1.1 This former coal miner, 77-year-old Saparbai Abdullaev, is among many thousands of workers in the former republics of the U.S.S.R. who have lost their livelihoods as the coal mining industry collapsed with the fall of the Soviet Union.

Unfortunately, as the year 2015 looms in the not-too-distant future, the goal of eradicating poverty still remains elusive. According to the United Nations Development Programme, 1.2 billion people in the world still live in extreme poverty, on less than $1 a day, while 2.8 billion live on less than $2 a day.[5] Like Bakyt, these people, who constitute nearly half of the world's population of 6.2 billion,[6] are terrified of the future, not knowing whether they'll be able to eat tomorrow, find work, or have a roof over their head.

What are the roots of this persistent poverty crisis in the world today? Is there hope for Bakyt and the billions of people like him? What effect does globalization have on poverty? What do globalization and poverty mean in the new millennium and how do these two phenomena interact?

Globalization is broadly defined as the trend toward a single, integrated, and interdependent world. As David Yergin explains in his impressive documentary *Commanding Heights: The Battle for the World Economy*, globalization is based on the freedom to trade, invest, communicate, and travel internationally.[7] It affects all major matters faced by humanity today, including poverty. This happens because, by opening their doors to the world, countries inevitably have to give up control over some portion of their economic, political, and social policies. Whereas in the past, government planning and economic policies were the primary drivers for a country's economic and social status, today much of it is left to the global economic forces, primarily the free market economy. In the past, poverty could easily be traced to the specific country's ill-conceived policies, government **corruption**, or other similar historical, cultural, or political reasons. In the era of globalization, the causes can be much more complex, diverse, and far-reaching, because many more external forces affect a country's fate. Therefore, today the relevant debate is whether poverty is yet another result of globalization or whether globalization is helping to solve the poverty crisis.

What makes matters more difficult to sort is that the notion of poverty has also evolved. **Poverty**, which in the past was assumed to mean the lack of money, was defined and categorized most recently in the 1995 Copenhagen Declaration of the World Summit for Social Development, signed by 117 countries. According to it, *absolute poverty* "is a condition characterized by severe deprivation of basic human needs, including food, safe drinking water, sanitation facilities, health, shelter, education, and information. It depends not only on income and productive resources but also on access to social services." The less extreme form, *overall poverty*, manifests itself in many different ways, including "lack of income and productive resources sufficient to ensure sustainable livelihoods; hunger and malnutrition; ill health; limited or lack of access to education and other basic services; increased morbidity from illness; homelessness and inadequate housing; unsafe environments; and social discrimination and exclusion.

It is also characterized by a lack of participation in decision-making and in civil, social and cultural life."[8] Despite these rather extensive definitions of poverty, academics, politicians, and business people continue to debate over the specific boundaries and measurements that regulate who is poor and who is not. Without going into too much detail, suffice it to say that standards are set differently in different countries, depending on the economic, social, and political systems in place. In developed countries, a higher income and **standard of living** would still be considered below the poverty line, while in developing countries, the same indicators would place someone above the poverty line.

Globalization as a Solution to Poverty

Many resources have been dedicated to eradicating poverty, especially within the leading **intergovernmental organizations (IGOs)** such as the World Bank, United Nations, and International Monetary Fund (IMF), also called **supranational organizations**. Additionally, numerous other governmental, private, and public foundations; academic institutions; philanthropists; and many ordinary citizens have devoted time, money, and efforts to find a solution to global poverty.

In many ways their efforts are paying off; the share of people living in extreme income poverty fell from 30 percent to 23 percent in the 1990s; China alone was able to see 150 million of its people rise above the poverty line; and more and more people are receiving small loans called micro-credits, enabling them to take control of their own destiny by starting a business or buying land.[9] In addition, life expectancy—the most basic and yet the most telling sign of improvement—has increased by 8 years in the developing world. Illiteracy, another major factor influencing poverty, decreased to half its previous levels, or 25 percent of the population.[10]

Globalization has also given voice and political clout to many indigenous people who, until recently, were forgotten, repressed, or exploited by their countries. This development is especially pronounced in Central and South America, where the president of Peru, Alejandro Toledo, is the first head of state with indigenous roots, and where activists such as the Nobel Prize winner Rigoberta Menchú are fighting for the rights of **indigenous people** on the world stage. Elsewhere, the Maoris in New Zealand, the Tlicho Indians and the Labrador Inuits in Canada, the rebels in the Chiapas region of Mexico, and the Ingorot in the Philippines are winning the battles for recognition, human rights, land ownership, and acknowledgment of other injustices their people have suffered in the advance of civilization. Their newly gained influence may not immediately solve the poverty, social exclusion, and exploitation plaguing these groups. There is no doubt, however, that globalization, by spreading democratic ideals and disseminating them through a multitude of activist groups who work with, recruit from, and fight for the agenda of indigenous people worldwide, has been a key factor in their advancement.[11]

Discussing globalization, author Daniel Yergin points out the crucial role of international trade in raising standards of living around the world. He gives as an example Singapore, which in only 35 years was able to transform itself from an extremely poor country to one where the **per capita income** is slightly higher than that of Britain—all thanks to opening its economy to the world market.[12] Despite success stories like these, much more remains to be done before globalization can be the undisputed solution to poverty.

Globalization as a Cause of Poverty

It is discouraging to think that the world has been fighting poverty in an organized, deliberate fashion for over 50 years, ever since the end of World War II and the disintegration of colonialism. The amount of money, food, and volunteers dedicated to helping poor nations over the years is staggering. So is the debt these countries owe to the World Bank, IMF, and other institutional lenders.[13] But the successes generated by these aid programs and **loan subsidies** are few and far between. According to the United Nations Development Program, if the goal to eradicate poverty is met, it will only be due to the great economic successes achieved in the two most populous nations—China and India. Not surprisingly, East Asia was the only region where the actual number of people in poverty declined significantly in the last ten years, while in sub-Saharan Africa, Eastern Europe, and the former Soviet Union, the number of poor people actually grew.[14]

Globalization's critics and dissenters blame it for many of the world's problems today, including persistent poverty. Many claim that the misguided economic policies and social programs of the World Bank, IMF, World Trade Organization (WTO), and similar organizations promote Western-style economics that only benefit the West while leaving people in developing countries worse off than they were before. Joseph Stiglitz, winner of the 2001 Nobel Prize in Economics, former World Bank chief economist, and author of one of the most influential anti-globalization books, *Globalization and Its Discontents*, puts it this way: "The Western countries have pushed poor countries to eliminate **trade barriers**, but kept up their own barriers, preventing developing countries from exporting their agricultural products and so depriving them of desperately needed export income." At the same time, Stiglitz argues, developed countries upheld their **trade quotas** on goods such as textiles and sugar, subsidized their agriculture, forced poor countries to lower their export prices, and allowed volatile **short-term investors** to reap the financial benefits of their speculations in developing countries before retreating and leaving the countries' currencies and banks in shambles.[15]

Anup Shah takes the argument further in his article "Structural Adjustment—A Major Cause of Poverty." In it, he claims that poor nations who are indebted to IGOs and the developed nations that finance them are required to make repaying their debts a priority at the expense of poverty-alleviating programs. Ultimately, these requirements, ranging from **trade liberalization**, to **exchange rate controls**, to market deregulation, reduce the standard of living of the people in these countries even more.[16]

Many similar arguments are made by a multitude of anti-globalization groups and individuals. No meeting of the World Bank, IMF, or WTO goes without loud and eloquent demonstrations that make their case against globalization as the cause for the widening gap between rich and poor, the destruction of communities, and the overall lowering of living standards for many developing nations.

Although the World Bank, IMF, and WTO dispute many of the above arguments, they are aware of the problems and the negative effects of their policies and have begun to make broad changes in their poverty eradication policies (*see* Chapter 7). Kenneth Rogoff, an economic counselor and director of the Research Department at the IMF, describes this new approach as "a more participatory approach, one that involves a country's government and its civil society at an early stage in measuring the size of the poverty problem and in devising development strategies to reduce poverty." He proudly notes that the new policies are receiving approval from some of globalization's staunchest critics, including Joseph Stiglitz.[17]

THE CAUSES OF POVERTY

Global poverty is a multidimensional and evolving phenomenon that touches on all aspects of human life in its personal, social, political, and economic contexts. It is hard to analyze because it is so inextricably linked to many other issues, such as hunger, gender, ethnicity, location, culture, and education. This interdependency makes it difficult to pinpoint poverty's exact causes (Figure 1.2). Nevertheless, the United Nations estimates that lack of money is still the main root of poverty, with illiteracy and lack of access to safe water close behind.[18] According to a more

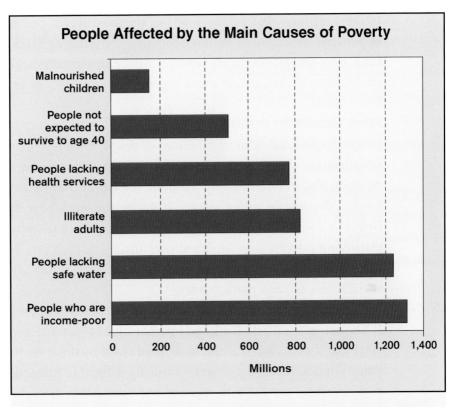

People Affected by the Main Causes of Poverty

Millions

Figure 1.2 Graph of the number of people affected by the main causes of poverty in 2000.

Source: United Nations Environment Programme, www.UNEP.net

abstract view, poverty is the result of the competition between different social groups for economic resources and political dominance. The losers in this competition end up with less food, less property, less income, and ultimately, less chance to reach the same levels of well being and human development as the winners.[19]

Major events such as wars, armed conflicts, and state economic crises; social phenomena such as corruption, bureaucracy, gender discrimination, environmental decline, and population growth; and, most of all, history, geography, and governance are causes of poverty around the world. However, it is important to note that all and any of these factors affect different countries in different ways. For example, one of the most recent causes of poverty, the acquired immunodeficiency syndrome (AIDS) epidemic, has affected sub-Saharan Africa in a much more profound way than in any other region.[20]

APPROACHES TO POVERTY

Poverty is personal. Although billions of people are affected by it, each one of them experiences poverty in a deeply unique way. Nevertheless, in order to help the poor, the world community has had to come up with a way to categorize and study poverty before it could start attacking it. Four major approaches to classifying poverty have emerged over the years, each one of them measuring a different aspect of it: monetary, capability, social exclusion, and participatory.[21]

The *monetary approach* is the most popular, especially among IGOs such as the World Bank and International Monetary Fund (IMF), and therefore it is the most publicized method. As its name implies, monetary poverty is usually defined in financial and economic terms, with income and consumption as the primary indicators. This approach is appealing to researchers because it uses easily measurable categories such as age, gender, income, household size, education level, health, and nutrition to define poverty. Although income and consumption levels can be used as a basis for defining some minimum standard for human deprivation, they often ignore the existence of free (and thus unmeasured) resources, such as social programs for health care or food self-sufficiency on a farm. The method relies heavily on previously measured values, such as the ubiquitously used poverty line which is defined as the minimum income needed to provide food, housing, clothing, medical care, etc. for a family. Defining this level of income, however, contains a degree of subjectivity. Overall, the monetary approach endorses a strategy for poverty alleviation that increases the incomes of the poor.

The much more conceptual *capability approach* regards poverty as the inability to reach a certain minimum level of human capability or well-being. While it expands the list of causes for poverty and rejects the utilitarianism of the monetary approach, the capability approach remains unclear on the definitions of the basic capabilities used to distinguish between poverty and non-poverty. This method advocates the use of more public goods and services but it is unable to completely avoid using money as one of the main tools for achieving quality of life.

Voices of the Poor

At the turn of the 21st century, the World Bank collected the voices of more than 60,000 poor women and men from 60 countries, in an effort to understand poverty from the perspective of the poor. *Voices of the Poor*, as this compilation is called, chronicles the aspirations and struggles of poor people for a life of dignity. Here are some excerpts:

"Poverty is like heat, you cannot see it. So to know poverty you have to grow through it."

—Adaboya, Ghana

"Poverty is lack of freedom, enslaved by crushing daily burden, by depression and fear of what the future will bring."

—Georgia

"For a poor person everything is terrible—illness, humiliation, shame. We are cripples; we are afraid of everything; we depend on everyone. No one needs us. We are like garbage that everyone wants to get rid of."

—a blind woman from Tiraspol, Moldova

"Poverty is like living in jail, living under bondage, waiting to be free."

—Jamaica

If you want to do something and have no power to do it, it is talauchi (poverty)."

—Nigeria

"When one is poor, she has no say in public, she feels inferior. She has no food, so there is famine in her house; no clothing, and no progress in her family."

—a woman from Uganda

Source: "Voices of the Poor—Listen to the Poor," World Bank. Available online at *http://www1.worldbank.org/prem/poverty/voices/index.htm.* Reprinted with permission.

Unlike the previous two approaches, the *social exclusion approach* goes beyond the individual and household unit to consider poverty as a social group phenomenon. It defines the poor as those who cannot participate in the normal practices of daily life for reasons out of their control. Typically, such groups include the elderly, handicapped, and the racially and ethnically disadvantaged. Although the social exclusion approach uses country-specific standards for defining poverty, it can be rather arbitrary and incomplete. It usually recommends social restructuring programs that enable inclusion of the poor back into society, such as a formal labor market.

Critics of the externally imposed measurements used in the monetary and capability approaches are usually proponents of the *participatory approach*, which asks the poor to define their situation themselves. By doing this, the method strives to empower the poor, increase the efficiency of the poverty alleviation programs, and stimulate mutual learning. One of the problems is that most participatory poverty assessments are conducted and interpreted by outsiders (such as World Bank employees) and thus their validity and accuracy is compromised. In addition, the subjectivity factor is high when people are asked to evaluate themselves.

Using these different approaches addresses the multidimensional aspects of poverty, but it also makes it more difficult to interpret the data and make decisions based on it. Most importantly, researchers have found that the different approaches often identify completely different social layers as poor, and therefore, recommend differing approaches to solving poverty. In one example, almost half of the population categorized as poor by using monetary poverty standards, was not covered under the capability poverty standards. The researchers conclude that a combination of all methods may be the most useful way to study the subject at hand. This new approach will further satisfy the move towards a broader, more inclusive definition of poverty.

THE GLOBAL ASPECTS OF POVERTY

The causes, symptoms and even the definitions of poverty vary greatly from country to country. Its effects are diverse and often puzzling. For example, in India poverty is high and unemployment is low, while in Morocco, poverty is not high, despite relatively high unemployment.[22] Its elusive nature notwithstanding, poverty remains a force that affects many aspects of the world we live in today.

The Global Poverty Report 2001 lists some of the vast and often ambiguous dynamics between globalization and poverty in five separate categories: (1) price of goods and services, (2) factors of production, (3) government resources, (4) economic growth, and (5) costs of transition.[23]

For example, when a country opens its markets and thus becomes more globalized, the prices of goods and services that are produced by the poor may change based on the global market demand for them. The same is true for the goods that poor people buy. Ideally, if the price of the goods produced goes up (due to more demand for it in the global market) and the price of goods consumed goes down (due to more supply), the poor would have more money in their pockets. Unfortunately, nothing is that simple when it comes to globalization and poverty. The prices of goods produced and consumed are affected by different factors and often move up or down independent of each other.

To see how factors of production can be affected, one only has to look at the labor outsourcing trend that has companies from more costly labor markets in the West (the United States and Western Europe) utilizing cheaper labor markets in the East (India, East Asia, and Eastern Europe). When a country with low labor prices globalizes, the price for its labor, especially for the more undesirable labor usually done by the poor, goes up due to the higher demand from overseas companies. Alas, this connection can be easily disrupted and even reversed by other factors such as technological advances that allow machines to do what was previously done by people or political instability that forces foreign investors to stay away from the country and its labor force.

A country's government revenue usually increases when many international investors, be they IGOs, businesses, or other governments, are allowed to invest in the country's economy. This extra income also means that the government has more money to spend on resources and programs for alleviating poverty. However, if the country does not manage its newly found capital properly (due to corruption, for example) or if it is negatively affected by globalization's market forces, the value of its currency weakens, for example.

On a greater scale, globalization tends to positively affect the **economic growth** of countries. A higher rate of economic growth also means more opportunities for all people in that country, including the poor. Nevertheless, growth is not a guarantee. For example, the World Bank's President, James Wolfensohn, points out that despite a 4 percent growth in 14 or 15 African countries in the last years, Africa continues to lose the battle on poverty.[24]

Finally, opening a country to the global market forces usually comes at a price. The costs of transition include high volatility in the political, economic, and social structures, often for years or even decades. During this period, many of the social safety nets (such as government subsidies and health benefits) needed by the poor are disrupted, leaving these most vulnerable members of society at the mercy of the markets.

The *Global Poverty Report* goes on to say that for trade reform to help reduce poverty, it has to be implemented together with the appropriate changes in the country's education and training systems, technology, investment, and infrastructure. And since such sweeping reforms have different results in different countries, regions, and social groups, it is difficult to determine the overall affects of globalization on poverty on a worldwide basis.

Many in the global community today believe that poverty greatly influences some of the negative trends of globalization. The Organization for Economic Co-operation and Development

(OECD) states that, "... in a rapidly globalizing world the social ills associated with poverty—disease, illicit migration, environmental degradation, crime, political instability, armed conflict and terrorism—can spread with greater ease across borders and continents." [25]

The only clear conclusion that emerges then, is that the interaction between poverty and globalization is multilayered, multidirectional, and a much more unpredictable phenomenon than expected. Fully understanding it and learning to control it will take much more time, resources, and commitment than currently available, according to outgoing World Bank President James Wolfensohn, who recently closed a conference dedicated to reducing poverty with the following remarks:

I believe that today lip service is given to the question of poverty. There are safe statements made by just about everybody about the issue of the Millennial Goals and about poverty. But the real issues today that seem to be on the mind of the world, terrorism, Iraq, Afghanistan, strains in the Trans-Atlantic Alliance, budget deficits, parochial problems, the visible problems that must be dealt with that are immediate, while attention is given less to the equally inevitable and the equally dangerous problems that come with poverty." [26]

Because the causes of poverty vary by region, in the following chapters we will take a closer look at the characteristics of poverty on the different continents of the world. As we have noted, poverty is also dependent on the economic, social, and political development of countries. Therefore, some chapters will deviate from their geographic organization: Chapter 4 will discuss the recent poverty trends in the new economic and political realities of Central and Eastern European countries and the former Soviet Union republics, while Chapter 6 will focus specifically on poverty in the developed countries of North America, Western Europe, and Australia.

Poverty in Africa

Africa, the birthplace of humanity and a continent rich in natural beauty and resources, as well as in an incredible human and cultural diversity, is currently the most desperate, poor, war-torn, and disease-torn place on earth. Despite persistent efforts by many local governments and the international community, Africa's social, economic, and political ills have increased in the last few decades, with very few signs of improvement in the near future. The continent's overwhelming poverty is both one of the main reasons and one of the main symptoms of Africa's unique situation. This chapter discusses the historical, ethnic, social, economic, and political contexts of poverty in the era of globalization. We consider primarily sub-Saharan Africa (SSA), the region where the problems and trends are most acute.

HISTORICAL PERSPECTIVES

Africa's history of poverty associated with oppression and exploitation is long and painful. For nearly 500 years, both European and Arab invaders saw Africa merely as a source of slave labor and natural resources. The enslavement of an estimated 10 million Africans[27] left the coastal regions of the continent largely depopulated and slowed down the natural progression of many local nations.[28]

For most of the 19th century, only the coastal regions of Africa were colonized and nearly 80 percent of all countries on the continent remained independent and locally governed (Figure 2.1). During the Berlin Conference of 1884–1885 however, fourteen European countries completely disregarded the **sovereignty** of the local peoples and forced colonial rule over a haphazardly divided Africa. France, Germany, Great Britain, and Portugal gained the most territories and political influence on the continent, which has been arbitrarily reshaped into new countries that ignored the ethnic, tribal, cultural, and linguistic differences long established among the African population.[29]

For the next nearly 80 years, the European powers plundered Africa's natural resources and exploited its people. By the time most countries regained their independence in the 1950s and 60s, the combined legacies of slavery and colonialism had left them poor and underdeveloped both socially and economically.[30]

Many Africans at the time considered poverty the result of their inability to own land and to access other productive resources and services during the colonial period. Freedom from colonialism therefore meant reclaiming political and economic control of their own countries and improving the plight of their own people. Some countries, such as Tanzania, Kenya, and Ghana made significant progress, as the former president of Tanzania, Julius Nyerere recalls in a recent interview:

> I was in Washington last year. At the World Bank the first
> question they asked me was 'How did you fail?' I responded that
> we took over a country with 85 per cent of its adult population
> illiterate. The British ruled us for 43 years. When they left, there
> were 2 trained engineers and 12 doctors. This is the country we
> inherited. When I stepped down there was 91% literacy and
> nearly every child was in school. We trained thousands of
> engineers and doctors and teachers. In 1988 Tanzania's per-
> capita income was $280.[31]

During the 1960s and 70s, the quality of life did indeed
better for many Africans. They had better access to water,
food, and health care; better educational opportunities; higher
literacy; lower infant mortality; and improved availability of
agricultural land and credit.

Even in the post-independence period, however, Africa was
unable to escape from foreign influences. Many of the newly
independent countries became battlegrounds for the two reign-
ing ideologies at the time, communism and capitalism.[32] Each
camp sought to impose its ideological and political stamp on as
much African territory as possible. Throughout the Cold War,
the East and the West continued to overtly or covertly manipu-
late events and policies and to influence African leaders. Many
countries adopted policies that stunted economic growth, and
allowed inefficiency and corruption to spread throughout
society. That development in turn triggered a gradual decline in
the standard of living, and, more importantly, left little resources
to help improve the plight of the already poor. Today, after
several decades of declining standards of living, the majority of
African people are worse off than they were at independence.[33]

ETHNIC PERSPECTIVES

Africa is home to over 680 million people who belong to more
than a thousand ethnic groups, distributed across over 50 countries. Some of these countries have over 20 different ethnicities

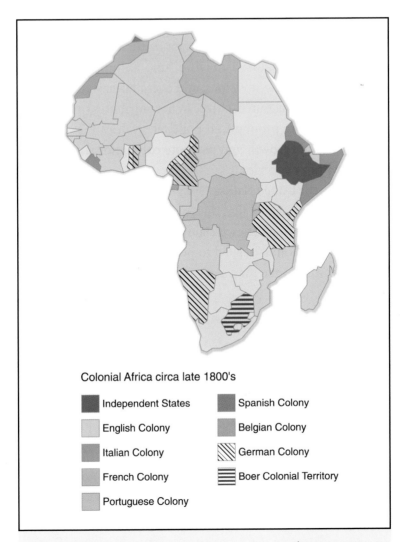

Colonial Africa circa late 1800's

■ Independent States		■ Spanish Colony	
■ English Colony		■ Belgian Colony	
■ Italian Colony		▧ German Colony	
■ French Colony		▤ Boer Colonial Territory	
■ Portuguese Colony			

Figure 2.1 Colonial Africa at the end of the 19th century. The colonial powers created many countries without regard for the history, ethnicity, language, or culture of the region.

living in their territories who speak a multitude of languages, practice diverse religions, and live different ways of life. From the Manding farmers in West Africa to the nomadic Khoikhoi in the South and the Dinka herders on the banks of the Nile, Africa is the most ethnically and linguistically diverse continent in the world today.[34]

Is diversity a blessing or a curse for Africa? While it is a veritable treasure chest of our human cultural heritage, Africa's diversity has also caused much ethnic animosity, sparking centuries of conflicts, invasions, and overall devastation. Ethnic diversity, according to recent research, contributes to less cooperation and more pronounced political rivalries that can slow down economic growth and promote corruption and political friction within countries.[35]

Although the United Nations-sponsored Human Development Report 2004 does agree that diverse societies tend to be poorer than homogenous societies, it claims that in Africa's case, the bad economic situation is "related to political decision-making that follows ethnic rather than national interests, not to diversity

African Languages

The number of distinctive languages spoken in Africa is open to debate. Some experts put the number at around 2,000, while others count more than 3,000. Virtually all of these languages originated in Africa. The most widely spoken indigenous African language is Swahili, spoken by nearly 50 million Africans, followed by Hausa and Yoruba, each with more than 20 million speakers. Several languages have only a few thousand speakers. Scholars generally recognize four African language families: Niger-Congo, Afro-Asiatic, Nilo-Saharan, and Khoisan.

Most Africans are multilingual, meaning that they speak two or more different languages. Few can afford to be otherwise, since daily life often brings people into contact with others who speak different languages. For instance, more than 50 languages are spoken in Nigeria alone. Tanzania, with significantly fewer people, has nearly 100 languages, including at least one from each of the four language families.

North Africans and converts to Islam have spoken Arabic for centuries, and the use of European languages has spread across the continent since the dawn of colonialism. Today, the language of a country's former colonial rulers often serves as its common tongue.

Source: "Africa," Microsoft® Encarta® Online Encyclopedia 2005. Available online at
http://encarta.msn.com/encyclopedia_761572628_8/Africa.html.

itself." It gives as a positive example Mauritius, a small island off Africa's southeastern coast, which, despite its ethnically and religiously diverse population of African, Indian, Chinese, and European descent, is the highest-ranked country from sub-Saharan Africa on the human development index.[36] The index ranks countries based on their level of development in three basic dimensions: life expectancy, literacy and income level.

The report goes on to recognize that ethnically driven politics can divide societies and endanger their peaceful development, especially when certain marginalized social groups resort to drastic political measures in order to defend their rights. This process is becoming more and more common in Africa, and indeed across the world, due to globalization and the rise of democratic values, communications, and human migration that it brings.

Cultural diversity and national unity don't have to be mutually exclusive, argues the report. Multi-ethnicity and peace can coexist if a society is open and inclusive.[37] Those are the prerequisites for building progressive countries that are united in the fight against poverty across racial, ethnic, and social boundaries.

ECONOMIC PERSPECTIVES

Professor George Saitoti, who has held various posts in Kenya's government and written extensively on African issues, suggests that the continent finds itself in the grip of poverty today because of several major errors in economic policies after independence, amongst other reasons. He claims that the momentum created in many African economies after the end of colonialism was unsustainable mostly because Africa's post-independence legal and economic frameworks were not designed to stimulate free enterprise and commercial activity. The indigenous population had no motivation to engage in productive labor, which caused a gradual decline in economic growth and standards of living across the continent. Further slowing the African economies was their governments' constant meddling with the free markets—by imposing controls over prices and interest rates, raising taxes, and taking over the management of agricultural production, for example. Such actions disrupted the creation of free market economies and prevented the generation and distribution of wealth that could have allowed people to get out of poverty.

During the 1980s, economic decline continued to spread across the African continent, spurred on by bloated and inefficient domestic industries and the trade policies such as import license requirements and foreign exchange restrictions designed to protect the industries from foreign competition. These limitations discouraged international commerce and, together with a series of other factors, such as oil crises, extensive national debt, and the **structural adjustment programs (SAPs)** imposed by the World Bank and IMF, contributed to the disastrous state of most African economies today.[38]

Other academics paint an even darker picture of Africa's economic situation. The renowned economist Jeffrey Sachs[39] and several of his colleagues suggest that bad governance and policies are not enough to explain the stagnant economies of many African countries. According to him, Africa is stuck in a "poverty trap, too poor to achieve robust, high levels of economic growth and, in many places, simply too poor to grow at all." Several factors have converged to create these conditions, including domestic savings that are too low to spur economic growth, lack of foreign investments in the countries to offset the low domestic funding, poor infrastructure, and poorly prepared people who are not able to join a modern work force without extensive training and education.

After discussing how sub-Saharan Africa fell into the poverty trap, Sachs explains why the region became so vulnerable to it in the first place. Of the five structural reasons offered, one is related to the historical issues discussed in the first section, another is social (and will be described in a subsequent section of this chapter), and three are economic: high transportation costs and small market size, low-productivity agriculture, and slow diffusion of technology from abroad.

High transportation costs are incurred because of the need to distribute goods to the interior parts of the continent, where most Africans live today. There, the soil is more fertile, the rains are more frequent, the threat of malaria is lower, and, in the past, the threat of being caught in the slave trade was lower. However, there are no navigable rivers for ships and few reliable or extensive roads for ground vehicles to bring goods to the population. What's more, the vast Sahara desert isolates the sub-Saharan region from its closest and major trading partner, Europe. These facts make transportation in Africa very expensive and contribute to the high costs of trade there. In addition, most African countries are small in size, making their markets less self-sustained and less attractive to international trade, especially when they are so hard to reach.

Another unfortunate combination of bad natural conditions (few irrigable rivers, not many fertile plains, and unreliable rainfall), and economic conditions (high transportation costs that raise the price of fertilizer to unaffordable levels for farmers), has made Africa the continent with the lowest share of irrigated cropland in the developing world. Such sparse and nutrients-depleted farmland produces little to feed the constantly growing African population. Compounding this problem is the persistent drought and civil conflicts that continue to disrupt life in many countries including Angola, Burundi, Congo, Senegal, Gambia, and Zimbabwe. Considering that, with the exclusion of South Africa, agriculture constitutes over 25 percent of SSA's **gross domestic product (GDP)**, it is easy to see how decreasing agricultural production also causes a decrease in the household incomes and food supplies for many Africans.[40]

Africa's agriculture could be much improved if only Africa were able to adopt technological advances more quickly. The so-called **green revolution** that swept through most of Latin America and Asia, providing scientifically modified high-yield varieties of crops, largely bypassed Africa. One of the reasons was that these crops were not suited to grow in the harsh climate and land conditions of sub-Saharan Africa. The other had to do with the added challenges of bringing irrigation and fertilizers to stimulate the adaptation of these crop varieties to the local environment. As a result, sub-Saharan Africa remains the region with the lowest cereal yield per hectare and the slowest gain in harvest over the last two decades. It is also the only major region in the world where less food was produced per capita during the period from 1980 to 2000 than before.

POLITICAL PERSPECTIVES

For nearly two decades after the independence movement, Africa's preferred method for changing the political land-scape of its countries was the brutal and disruptive military **coup d'etat**, the overthrow of a legal government by force. These political shocks not only created an atmosphere of instability and uncertainty, they also replaced many young democratic systems with authoritarian regimes and even dictatorships. Such national crises did little to contribute to the people's well-being and the creation of social networks to fight poverty.

According to Dr. Saitoti, Africa's institutions and governments were not designed to prevent the massive abuses of public trust, power, and responsibility by politicians and bureaucrats that have become common since the post-independence period.[41] No system of checks and balances was installed to stop these elected officials from violating their mandates, taking bribes, and engaging in other opportunistic behaviors. In this sense, the African states failed to provide their citizens with the three basic functions expected from governments: the provision of economic freedom, the constraint of state custodians, and the enhancement of peaceful coexistence of population groups.

African workers face an unstable business and political system that is full of cronyism, bureaucracy, corruption, and ethnic discrimination. Such an environment cannot stimu-late entrepreneurship and the work ethic, two of the major requirements needed to create business opportunities and deal effectively with poverty.

Although well intended, external policies designed by the major IGOs further contributed to the political chaos in Africa. The structural adjustment policies (SAPs) that were intended to ensure the repayment of debt by developing nations were perceived by Africans as just "another form of colonialism," according to Dr. Saitoti. Furthermore, the programs did not take into account the unique circumstances in each country and failed to gain acceptance in many communities and social groups. Their spotty implementation forced many governments to divert funds originally intended for social programs and poverty reduction towards debt repayment, which caused a sizeable backlash and accelerated Africa's downward spiral in living standards.

SOCIAL PERSPECTIVES
Disease Epidemics

Perhaps the biggest social problem facing Africa today is its enormous disease burden. Africa is a continent ravaged by fatal diseases such as AIDS, malaria, and tuberculosis. Whereas people can expect to live to an average of 77 years in the United States, the life expectancy of African people is only 50 years and even less than 40 years in some of the countries most devastated by AIDS.[42] In these countries, including Botswana, Lesotho, Namibia, South Africa, and Swaziland, AIDS has claimed over 20 percent of the adult population. Overall, Africa is home to two-thirds of the total number of people in the world living with HIV, despite the fact that it comprises only 10 percent of the world's population (Figure 2.2).[43]

Even more disconcerting is the fact that due to the AIDS pandemic 11 million of the continent's children are orphans and the number is expected to rise exponentially.[44] The immediate impact of the AIDS crisis on poverty is evident in the increased burden placed on extended families who most frequently become the caregivers for the orphans: their household income

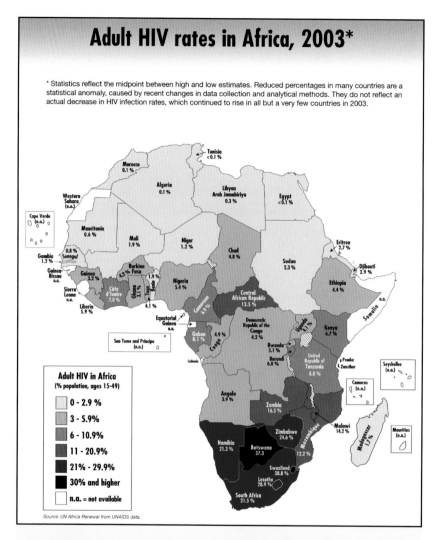

Adult HIV rates in Africa, 2003*

* Statistics reflect the midpoint between high and low estimates. Reduced percentages in many countries are a statistical anomaly, caused by recent changes in data collection and analytical methods. They do not reflect an actual decrease in HIV infection rates, which continued to rise in all but a very few countries in 2003.

Adult HIV in Africa
(% population, ages 15-49)

- 0 - 2.9 %
- 3 - 5.9%
- 6 - 10.9%
- 11 - 20.9%
- 21% - 29.9%
- 30% and higher
- n.a. = not available

Source: UN Africa Renewal from UNAIDS data.

Figure 2.2 Africa is home to the majority of the people in the world with HIV, although it is home to only 10 percent of the world population.

Source: *Africa Renewal* magazine, "Silent No More: Fighting HIV/AIDS in Africa" (*www.un.org/AR*)

usually diminishes by 31 percent, effectively making these families the poorest of the poor. The ripple effects of this catastrophic trend will be felt for years to come as high mortality wipes out major parts of the work force and tests the strengths of social structures and economies.

Adding to the disease burden are two other major diseases common in Africa, malaria and tuberculosis. Malaria kills 1 to 3 million Africans, 90 percent of them in the sub-Saharan Africa region. One in five people affected by tuberculosis in the world also live in Africa, and another 200 million Africans carry the disease.[45] In a discussion paper for the Brookings Institution, Jeffrey Sachs and his coauthors explain how malaria adds to Africa's poverty trap:

> With enough investment, even Africa's high malaria morbidity and mortality could be controlled, although not eliminated, with current technologies. But that would require substantially more money than Africa can afford. Thus Africa is too poor to control malaria, and meanwhile malaria reduces productivity, frustrates foreign investment, and (by contributing to very high child mortality rates) delays or stops the demographic transition, thereby helping to keep Africa poor.[46]

Population Growth

It is widely accepted that the size, growth rate, age composition, and the rural or urban distribution of the population in a given country greatly affect its chances for successful poverty eradication and economic progress. Poverty and overpopulation are parts of a vicious cycle that is also responsible for persistent health problems and gender discrimination.[47] Nowhere are these symptoms more pronounced than in sub-Saharan Africa. United Nations Population Fund statistics show that the region has the highest fertility rate in the world—5.5 children per woman— along with some of the highest mortality for mothers.[48]

A drastic population increase continues despite the AIDS epidemic and the growing awareness among African women of the negative economic consequences of having too many children. One of the main reasons for the growth rate is the lack of contraceptives, while others include the absence of family planning services, education, and cultural and ethnic traditions. [49]

Whatever the reasons, the net effect of having too many people in a country with too little resources to sustain them is deepening poverty, less access to health services and education, and more environmental devastation.

Displacement of People

Africa leads the world in another sad statistic: internal displacement of people. More than half of the people in the world who had to leave their homes forcibly in 2003 were in Africa (13 million of an estimated 23 million worldwide). Most of them were forced to abandon their villages due to armed conflicts. Civil wars, rebel movements, and ethnically charged clashes for political or economic dominance caused millions of people to live on the run or in crowded relief camps set up by the international organizations in countries such as Angola, the Democratic Republic of Congo, Sudan, Uganda, Liberia, and the Central African Republic.[50] Another 3 to 4 million Africans are classified as refugees because they have crossed into other, usually neighboring countries.[51] Few can forget the horrors of Rwanda, where in the early 1990s, over 800,000 were killed and another 2 million became refugees from an ethnically charged war, or the current situation in the Darfur region of Sudan, where over 50,000 have been killed as of October 2004 and hundreds of thousands have been chased out of their villages, all in a government-sponsored campaign of genocide.

Sometimes, food scarcity or natural disasters push people to leave. As author Daniel Cohen points out in his book *The Wealth of the World and the Poverty of Nations*, "[t]he displacement of peasants from their land, a thing of the past in rich countries, is still at a very early stage in poor countries."[52] Although Africa's economy is still very much dependent on agriculture, many farmers are forced to leave their land because of constantly diminishing crops, declining prices for their produce, persistent droughts, and other natural or man-made obstacles to making a living in Africa's rural environment.

When so many people are forced to migrate they become dependent on state or social organizations for the provision of food, shelter, health care, and so on. Such emergency situations often exhaust even further the already few available resources earmarked for long-term poverty solutions.

CURRENT TRENDS

Our world is dangerously out of kilter when a few hundred people in the United States command more income than 166 million people in Africa.
    —Jeffrey D. Sachs, The *New York Times*, July 9, 2003.

Solving the problem of chronic poverty has become the most important goal for Africa and the world community. Before any economic growth and long-term boost to the standards of living can be achieved, the countries of sub-Saharan Africa have to tackle many of the obstacles related to poverty such as the burden of heavy malnutrition and disease, poor education, deep corruption, vast inequality in incomes, ethnic hatred, political instability, and the many other tentacles of deep social devastation that have engulfed the continent for decades.

Africa's potential in the world stage can be glimpsed from the few encouraging developments there in the last couple of years. For example, the average per capita income rose in 2002 for a fourth year in a row, constituting the longest continuous rise since the 1970s. The growing international authority and stabilizing influence of institutions such as the African Union, New Partnership for Africa's Development, and the East African Community is also a great step forward. Furthermore, some unique programs such as the U.S. African Growth and Opportunities Act (AGOA) have demonstrated Africa's potential in non-traditional exports. More specific success stories have occurred in South Africa, which was the fastest-growing tourist destination in the world for 2002, and in several oil-producing nations such as Nigeria, Gabon, Lesotho, and Kenya, which have seen their exports to the United States increase substantially under AGOA.[53]

In fact, the oil boom currently underway in several African countries provides a momentous opportunity for the continent to change course toward economic growth and globalization. As the United States and other nations are set to pour billions of dollars into the development of oil-extraction infrastructure and trade in the west coast region of Africa, the affected countries' governments, the IGOs operating there, and the oil companies must act with utmost responsibility, transparency, and ethics to ensure that the influx of capital will be used to the benefit of the largest and the most disadvantaged group of people in the world—Africa's poor.[54]

Poverty in Asia

Development, diversity, and disparity—all three terms can be applied to the process of globalization and the fight against poverty in the vast continent of Asia. From the booming hybrid economy of China and the myriad developing countries in Southeast Asia, to the rising star of India, the newly independent republics of Central Asia, and the restless Middle East, this part of the world is a patchwork of cultural, economic, social, and political systems. Only a regional and even country-specific approach will allow an adequate look at the progress of globalization and the plight of the poor in the developing countries of Asia. Although it takes up a considerable part of Asia's territory, Russia will be discussed in the chapter on Europe, while North African countries such as Egypt, Morocco, Libya, and Algeria will be included in this chapter's section on the Middle East, due to their cultural, religious, and economic similarities with that region.

EAST ASIA AND THE PACIFIC

The developing countries of East Asia and the Pacific region were considered some of the best examples of globalization's positive effects on poverty for the last few decades. Following in the steps of the so-called Asian Tigers—Singapore, Hong Kong, and Taiwan, countries such as Indonesia, Malaysia, South Korea, and China adopted broad market-oriented economic reforms and began integrating into global trade. This process involved the complex task of transitioning from largely agricultural economies to more exports-based and industrialized production. The results of this transformation have been spectacular, according to the World Bank: in the last 30 years, more people got out of poverty in these four countries than in all other developing countries combined.[55] China, Indonesia, Malaysia, and South Korea shine in all basic indicators of improved quality of life: they have achieved higher life expectancy, lower infant mortality, more children in school, and fewer poor people, and they made this progress faster than any other developing countries.

How were these nations able to achieve such great success? The answer, according to the researchers from the World Bank's Poverty Reduction and Economic Management Network, is that these countries were able to reach a state where there is fast and yet sustainable growth, prosperity is shared across social layers, and the government institutions are unbiased and transparent. Although each country arrived at this state by different means, they all had certain elements in common, such as emphasis on exports, education, job creation, and private investments and a stable national economic climate. The cumulative effect of these changes has been that the poorest 40 percent of the population have seen their income grow faster than the overall economic rate for their countries.[56]

As is to be expected, this rosy picture has its detractors. For example, a 2001 report by the Organization for Economic Co-operation and Development (OECD) claims that for many other East Asian countries, income distribution and poverty eradication has not been equal or problem-free since the 1990s.[57] Furthermore, the report suggests that income distribution patterns indicate other problematic issues such as ethnic and gender discrimination and geographic differences that have become even more pronounced in the years after the 1997 currency crisis in the region. For example, in Thailand, the poverty rate continued to go up together with the economic growth rate between 1975 and 1985, while in the Philippines, the rate remained stable, but twice as high as the rest of the region. Disparities in the poverty levels of the population in urban and rural areas, in the different regions of the countries, and in different ethnic groups were also found to be significant.

The relationship of ethnicity to poverty is central in Amy Chua's book *World on Fire: How Exporting Free Market Democracy Breeds Ethnic Hatred and Global Instability.* In it, she argues that a quick transition to a democratic free-market system often propels a certain ethnic group to economic dominance over the rest, which sparks domestic animosity and conflicts. Such "market-dominant minorities" rise to prominence during the most crisis-prone and economically critical period of a country's transition. Chua gives as examples the Philippines and Indonesia, where ethnic Chinese control most of the countries' private business sectors despite being only 1 to 3 percent of the populations. Such huge disparities in income and influence are often the result of corruption and cronyism (among other factors), as was the case in Indonesia, where the Chinese minority collaborated to keep General Suharto in power so he can continue to dole out preferential treatment and political favors to its members. In 1998, the obvious inequalities and injustices toward the native Indonesians erupted in widespread protests and riots that forced Suharto to resign.[58]

Another notable fact is that the poverty lines drawn by the World Bank may not be adequate for measuring poverty in the region. For example, the Asian Developing Bank points out that when using the $1-day standard for extreme poverty, Indonesia's poor constitute only 7.5 percent of the population. However, when the $2 a day poverty standard is used, a whopping 52 percent of the population falls in the category.[59] In addition, the sheer size of the population in China, for example, brings the number of extremely poor to an over-whelming 200 million, although that number represents "only" 17 percent of that country's population (Figure 3.1).[60]

China's only remaining communist ally in the region, North Korea, represents another dilemma: its self-imposed isolation from the world and a decade of economic ruin has turned a large part of its population into the extremely impoverished, surviving on insects and plants, according to an eyewitness report for the CBS TV program *60 Minutes*.[61] Relief organizations estimate that in 2003, over 60 percent of North Korea's children were malnourished. An urgent request for more food aid to the country from the UN-led World Food Program in October 2004 shows that the situation has not improved.[62] Chronic malnutrition; limited access to safe water, medical service, or electricity; topped off with a constant and militant communist propaganda in the state-controlled media has turned this nation of 22 million people into ghosts—unseen and unheard of, except for their leader, Kim Jong Il, who is currently negotiating with the West for more food and financial aid based on the threat of North Korea's nuclear weapons.

Despite the remaining issues, the experts agree that China and most of Southeast Asia will "comfortably meet the first MDG [Millennium Development Goal] target under the assumption that current growth rates continue . . . ."[63] It is a tenuous, but nevertheless encouraging statement for the millions of poor in East Asia.

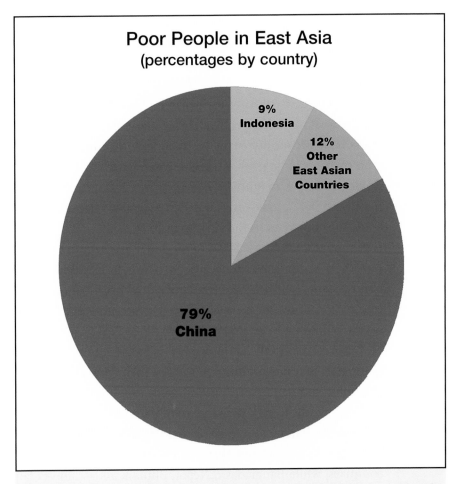

Poor People in East Asia
(percentages by country)

9%
Indonesia

12%
Other
East Asian
Countries

79%
China

Figure 3.1 The number of poor people in a country should be considered in proportion to the total population of that country. China, with a population of over 1 billion and Indonesia, with over 200 million, are the two most populous countries in East Asia and have the highest number of poor people.

Source: "Facts about East Asian Vulnerability and Poverty," by Tamar Manuelyan Atinc, World Bank.

SOUTH ASIA

South Asia contains India, the other industrial giant on the continent besides China. Just like China, India's promise as a substantial global power is evident in the statements of Thomas Friedman, the popular *New York Times* journalist and author of *The Lexus and the Olive Tree*, who, upon return from a trip to India remarked, "It's a country that really is hard wired basically to take advantage educationally, culturally, in terms of democracy and secularism, really to take advantage of the 21st century."[64]

While India is starting to realize its potential in cities like Bangalore, the Indian equivalent of the Silicon Valley, such pockets of prosperity seem far away for the country's poor, who live predominantly in rural areas (Figure 3.2). India and its South Asian neighbors need to find a way to translate high economic growth in the urban areas into better poverty eradication policies in the rural areas.[65]

Although India has achieved a modest, but steady decrease in poverty over the last two decades, progress in Nepal has been almost static, while the contradictory data from national and international poverty surveys of Bangladesh and Pakistan indicate it is difficult to establish clear trends in those countries.[66]

A report by the OECD points out that while the countries in South Asia may have a common history, their current economic and political situations are quite different.[67] Politically, the group runs the gamut from a parliamentary democracy (India) to an absolute monarchy (Bhutan). India, Pakistan, and Sri Lanka's economic indicators put them in the category of developing countries, while Bangladesh, Nepal, Bhutan, and Maldives fall under the unfortunate sub-category of least developed countries (LDC). Nevertheless, most South Asian countries experienced a marked economic improvement in the 1990s and continue to show over 5 percent growth per year. How was it that this substantial economic progress did not help the region's 400 million poor? The answers from the OECD researchers suggest that South Asia was not quick enough to follow its fiscal, financial, and banking reforms with a wave of institutional reforms that would have ensured that the resources generated by the economic progress were used to alleviate poverty on a mass scale.[68]

Other barriers holding down the poor in South Asia include the lack of access to safe water, food, education, health services,

Figure 3.2 India's poverty issues seem far away from the booming IT (information technology) centers in Bangalore, the Indian Silicon Valley. Employees of 24/7 Customer in Bangalore provide telephone support for clients in the United States and the United Kingdom and must work through the night.

gender equality, and other basic human necessities.[69] Nowhere else is the issue of child labor as pressing as in South Asia, where millions of children in countries such as Nepal, India, and Bangladesh toil in the mining, stone-cutting, construction, and textile industries, and thousands of others serve as soldiers in countries such as Sri Lanka and Afghanistan.[70] Armed conflicts, such as the continuing struggle between the Taliban, regional warlords, and the newly democratic forces in Afghanistan, or the stand off between Pakistan and India over disputed territories constitute another major obstacle to poverty reduction efforts in the region.

Nevertheless, it is encouraging that South Asian countries seeking foreign investment and aid are now required to submit **Poverty Reduction Strategy Papers** to the international lending institutions. The countries' plans for regional economic cooperation and targeted learning from their East Asian neighbors are also steps in the right direction. Only through such purposeful progressive strategies can South Asia win the poverty eradication war.

CENTRAL ASIA

Comprised of six former USSR republics (Azerbaijan, Kazakhstan, Kyrgyzstan, Tajikistan, Turkmenistan, and Uzbekistan), and with Mongolia often added in, the Central Asian region is still reeling from the dissolution of the Soviet Union in 1991 and the economic and political shocks that followed this momentous event.

Geographically isolated, historically marginalized, and economically disadvantaged, these countries had the highest poverty rates under the communist regime of the former Soviet Union.[71] Their economies, which were tightly controlled by Moscow and concentrated primarily in the cotton, agriculture, and oil production industries, did not make the transition from central planning to open markets easily. Most of the countries suffered exorbitant **inflation** and **recessions** in the early 1990s, which only exacerbated the plight of the poor and swelled their ranks.

The transition to a **market economy**, the loss of the Soviet Union as their major trading partner, and the resulting economic crisis disturbed the relative income equality that was typical of these countries in the communist era. The existence of social strata based on wealth has become apparent in the last decade. According to a recent survey by the OECD, the factors deciding how most Central Asians were affected by the crisis were family size, age, education level, and location. The most negatively affected have been large families with many children and the pensioners—groups most dependent on the social services of the state for **income supplements**. People with college-level education tend to have a higher income level than the rest, and people in certain geographic regions of each country tend to be more prosperous than in other regions.[72] The geographic differences may be explained by the historically distinct lifestyles led by the more nomadic Kyrgyz, Kazakhs, and Turkmens on one hand and the more urban, settled Uzbeks and Tajiks on the other.[73]

A more disturbing development is the increased and persistent poverty among children in the region, which has been linked to an increase in the number of intravenous drug users, especially in Kyrgyzstan and Kazakhstan. According to UNICEF, over half of the children in Kyrgyzstan, for example, still live below the national poverty line.[74]

It is important to note that, although a higher standard for poverty ($2 a day) is used in this region, its advantages are negated by the fact that the local poor have to spend extra on heating and clothing in the harsh winters there.[75] Equally significant is the fact that much of the data is outdated or intermittent, especially for Mongolia, where the best estimates indicate that poverty there has increased significantly in the mid- to late 1990s.[76]

In the last few years, more and more of the Central Asian countries have come to the conclusion that going it alone, with their small domestic markets, tattered infrastructure, and narrow trade relationships, will only prolong the painful transition period. Therefore, with assistance from the Asian Development Bank, seven countries (Azerbaijan, Kazakhstan, Kyrgyzstan, Mongolia, Tajikistan, Uzbekistan, and the People's Republic of China—focusing on Xinjiang Uyger Autonomous Region) have agreed to join in a Central Asia Regional Economic Cooperation (CAREC) program as their most efficient and expedient way for improving the region's well-being and allowing its integration into the global economy.[77]

MIDDLE EAST

The United States became much more familiar with the Middle East after the events of September 11, 2001. Once known primarily for its rich oil reserves, the region in the last few years has become synonymous with terrorism, radical Islamic clerics, and the war in Iraq. Unfortunately, the Middle East and the North African countries of Algeria, Egypt, Libya, Morocco, and Tunisia, which are usually included as part of it, hold another dark secret: the widespread poverty of their populations.

In its first-ever study on the status of human development in the Middle East, a team of Arab scholars and specialists working under the auspices of the United Nations set out to find out why the region has not been able to fully take advantage of its inherent potential. Published in 2002, the *Arab Human Development Report* notes that "[t]he Arab region has dramatically reduced poverty and inequality in the 20th century. It can do so again in the 21st century."[78]

When looked at from a purely statistical perspective, the Middle East did indeed improve the plight of its people in the last 30 years in some basic indicators such as life expectancy (up by 15 years) and infant mortality (reduced by nearly 75 percent). The population living on less than $1 a day is smaller than in any other developing region.[79] But below the surface of these encouraging facts is a different story. A persistent stagnation has set in over the last 20 years for per capita income and productivity indicators, resulting in a decline in the actual worker wages and dragging more and more people into poverty. The report estimates that 25 percent of Arabs still live on less than $2 a day. Furthermore, the region's high population growth and its youthful demographics (nearly 40 percent of Arabs are under the age of 14) spell disastrous unemployment rates in the future if more opportunities and education are not created for the new generations.[80]

"What went wrong with the Arab world?" asks an article in *The Economist* discussing the United Nations report.[81] It answers its own question by pointing out that "with barely an exception, its autocratic rulers, be they presidents or kings, give up their authority only when they die, its elections are a sick joke, half its people are treated as lesser legal and economic beings, and more than half its young, burdened by joblessness and stifled by conservative religious tradition, are said to want to get out as soon as they can." These factors boil down to what the *Arab Human Development Report* finds are the three key deficits in the region's progress: freedom, women's empowerment, and knowledge.[82] If the Middle East is to fulfill the potential of its abundant resources, it will have to first eliminate the restrictions for these three major milestones for progress (Figure 3.3).

Aside from such strategic and future-oriented recommendations, the Arab world is still left to deal with the immediate issues of poverty and hunger among its people. A recent assessment by the World Bank that was based on nationally defined poverty lines, show the number of poor in some North African countries, such as Mauritania and the tiny Djibouti, at 46 percent and nearly 80 percent, respectively.[83] Yemen, with the number of poor at 40 percent, and Algeria and Morocco, at around 20 percent, are also struggling with poverty. An even more current report (2004) covering the region cites a 9 percent poverty rate in Syria, and rates of 15 percent in Jordan, 26 percent in Egypt, and 30 percent in Lebanon.[84]

It is likely, however, that even these statistics are skewed, due to several issues specific to the region: first, many of the countries there have been under-researched[85]; second, the cultural and religious traditions promote charity; and third, close family ties often prevent those most at risk from slipping into poverty.[86] The last two factors, extrapolated from a report focusing on Saudi Arabia's progress on the UN's Millennium Development Goals, are followed by the observation that the government's extensive welfare policies also contribute to the relatively low poverty level in the Kingdom.

In all Arab states, rural poverty is significantly higher than urban poverty. Unfortunately, poverty in all areas is likely to increase unless the region finds a way to integrate the

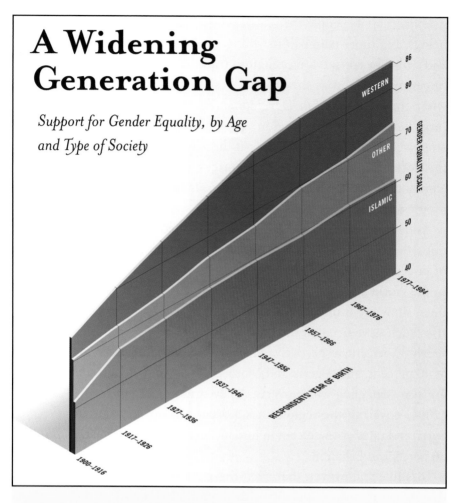

A Widening Generation Gap

Support for Gender Equality, by Age and Type of Society

Figure 3.3 Although younger Muslims express more support for gender equality than the older generations, Islamic societies still rank the lowest in their support for women's rights.

Source: Ronald Inglehart and Pippa Norris, "The True Clash of Civilizations," *Foreign Policy*, March/April 2003, p.72.

poor into society and create many new jobs, concludes the World Bank.[87]

Development Trends for the Future of Asia

"With concerted efforts, Asian countries have freed themselves from the shadow of the financial crisis, overcome the

*impact of SARS and bird flu, succeeded in domestic eco-
nomic restructuring, and quickened the tempo of industrial
upgrading and transformation, promoted a robust regional
cooperation, and increased the capacity to tide over potential
risks. Asia retains its position as one of the world's most
dynamic regions and a key growth point in global trade. All
these have given us much confidence in Asia's future."*

—Hu Jintao, President of China
24 April, 2004[88]

What does the future hold for Asia's developing countries? As
this analysis has shown, each of the continent's regions has
its own set of strengths and weaknesses and deals with its own
challenges in unique ways. How will the first democratically
elected president of Afghanistan deal with the devastating
poverty in that country? Is war-torn Iraq going to follow in
Afghanistan's footsteps or will it disintegrate into further chaos
and despair after the foreign troops leave? Can India find a way
to channel the fruits of its newly found success in the global
information-technology arena into the dirt-floor shacks of its
remote villages? Will China's success in managing economic
growth translate into better human rights for its people? Is
Iran's nuclear program going to further destabilize the already
volatile Middle East?

Wired Villages—a plan to bring the Net to rural India

The Dhar district of central Madhya Pradesh state is a microcosm of India's
deep poverty. More than half of Dhar's population of 1.7 million are illiterate
Bhil tribal farmers who live in thatched-roof huts and subsist on an average
of $270 a year. It hasn't rained in Dhar in three years.

Nevertheless, thanks to a government-backed program called Gyandoot,
or "ambassador of knowledge," Dhar is at the center of a grassroots
technology revolution that could spread around the world. Since January,
2000, Gyandoot has installed 39 computer kiosks at different locations

around Dhar that have electronically connected some 1 million villagers to the wider world. For the equivalent of 1 cent, kiosk staff tap farmers into a server at the Dhar chief administrator's office that allows them to check current prices for produce. For a few cents more, villagers can obtain land records, driver's licenses, and even school exam results online. Or they can look up disease-prevention tips for livestock. The local kiosk operators create new businesses, too. They buy the PCs through local bank loans, then use the computers to offer other services, such as selling PC lessons to local children. Dhar's total investment in the network: $73,000.

The payoff in poverty reduction could be dramatic. Consider the impact on Bahadur Singh Katare. Before Gyandoot arrived, he traveled 10 miles each week during harvest seasons to Dhar's main market to sell his soybeans for $16.60 per 100 kilograms [220 pounds], sharing a cut with a middleman. Now Katare, 23, first travels five miles to the kiosk in the village of Tirla to check prices nationwide. Last year, he found his soybeans would fetch $20.80 in Indore. He hired a truck and took 2,500 kilos [5,512 pounds] to Indore, an hour away, and boosted his net income 18%. "There are lots of people like me," says Katare, beaming.

Indeed there are. A villager in Gunawad auctioned his cow over Gyandoot for a profit. Pensioners who hadn't received their $3.12 monthly payment for four months sent an e-mail complaint, and the problem was rectified by the state three days later. Small enterprises that normally endure endless red tape to get a bank loan now get them in a month because documents are processed online. Others get quick access to land records necessary to get loans, collect an inheritance, or sell property. Indian villagers who cannot tap digital technology must travel hundreds of miles to state capitals.

Gyandoot isn't trouble-free. Power and phone connections are unreliable. So Dhar is experimenting with solar panels and local wireless networks in some areas. Local officials are eager to improve service because they now are peppered with e-complaints. "People have become more vocal in their demands," says Dhar district administrator Sanjay Dube, who also runs Gyandoot. "Since they are paying for services, they expect us to respond." For the long-neglected rural poor of India—and the world—technology may help pave the road out of poverty.

Source: Manjeet Kripalani, "Wired Villages: A Plan to Bring the Net to Rural India," *Business Week*, October 14, 2002. Available online at *http://www.businessweek.com/ magazine/content/02_41/b3803608.htm.*

These immediate questions only scratch the surface of some of the larger themes pertinent to Asia's future, such as population growth, environmental sustainability, and ethnic and religious diversity. None of these issues are easy to tackle, but through a continued emphasis on regional cooperation, economic growth, and equal distribution Asia is likely to move forward. The people of Asia have proven time and again that with good planning, shared goals and efforts, and persistence, any country can become an Asian Tiger.

Poverty in Europe

With its generally high standard of living, Europe does not typically come to mind as one of regions affected by poverty. Since the fall of communism in the countries of Central and Eastern Europe (CEE) and the former Soviet Union, however, these developing countries have been grappling with the issues of poverty for the first time in over 50 years.

BACKGROUND

Poverty was not something common or expected in the CEE countries and the European part of the Commonwealth of Independent States (CIS), which includes Armenia, Belarus, Georgia, Moldova, Russia, and Ukraine. These countries were the only ones in the world that saw their societies go from virtually no poverty in the late 1980s to a precipitous fall into poverty for 25 percent to 30 percent and more of their populations in the 1990s. During the last decade of the 20th century, this region experienced the fastest growing rate of poverty in the world.[89]

The causes of this massive regional crisis are well known by now: the fall of communism, the disintegration of the Soviet Union and its economic network, the sudden transitions from planned to market-based economies, the outdated industrial complex and a work force poorly prepared for the rigors of entrepreneurship and global competition.

Looking back, it is clear to some of the main architects of this transition that the impending poverty crisis should have been anticipated and possibly prevented. In a paper issued in 2000 and quoted in the 2004 *Economies in Transition* report, the World Bank acknowledges that "[t]he general expectation was that poverty was limited, and ... very shallow. The presumption was that growth would come quickly [and that] it would reduce the incidence of poverty rapidly. Poverty was believed to be largely transitory in nature, and best addressed through the provision of adequate safety nets."[90]

Many in these countries still have not transitioned out of poverty and there were no safety nets left to catch them from falling into it in the first place. The unanticipated and sudden breakdown of the main trading partner, supplier of basic resources, and financier for the CEE states—the Soviet Union— sent these countries reeling. Virtually all countries in the region experienced a shock that reverberated to their core: public sector spending was deeply reduced, industrial production stopped, trade on local, national, and international levels disappeared.[91] The effect on the people was equally devastating. In the early 1990s, only one in 25 people in the region lived on less than $2 a day, but in 2002, close to one in 5 did.[92]

Poverty in Central and Eastern Europe and the Commonwealth of Independent States is unique also because it does not fit the typical profile of poverty in most of the rest of the world. The phenomenon is usually and historically associated with lack of basic food and water supplies, low education, and employment insecurities. However, in this region until recently, food and water were never lacking, education was free and available to all, and employment was virtually guaranteed for life by the state. To this day, the majority of the poor in the region are literate and employable.[93]

REGIONAL CHARACTERISTICS OF POVERTY

Although virtually all formerly communist states in Europe transitioned to one form of democracy or another at around the same time (1989 to 1991), they are at different stages of economic development today. The success of the Czech Republic, Estonia, Hungary, Latvia, Lithuania, Poland, the Slovak Republic, and Slovenia is evident in their admission to the European Union on May 1, 2004. Other countries, however, continue to struggle with reform, a fact that is reflected in the high levels of poverty in Moldova, Romania, and Albania, where over 20 percent of the population still lives on less than $2 a day.[94]

Central Europe and the Baltic States

A combination of factors allowed the Central European and Baltic states to recover relatively quickly from the shock of transition from communism to democracy. Their historically closer ties with Western Europe and Scandinavia allowed them to restore trade relations faster, their central location within Europe and/or their access to the Baltic Sea facilitated commerce and transportation, and their quicker adoption to structural and **fiscal reforms** provided the necessary framework for economic growth, while their well-educated work force became a convenient and cheaper alternative for foreign businesses that wanted to establish a base in these promising markets. Furthermore, the **free trade areas** created among the countries of both Central Eastern Europe and the Baltic created an important proving ground for the abilities of these countries for intraregional trade cooperation and a much needed alternative to the growing dependency on Western Europe as a main trade partner.[95]

As a result, Central Europe and the Baltic countries are showing better economic performance and lower poverty levels than most other countries in Europe.[96] Nevertheless, problems remain. According to the United Nations Development Programme (UNDP), even in the most advanced Central European nations of Hungary, the Czech Republic, the Slovak Republic, and Slovenia, the ranks of the poor continue to grow among minorities, women, and large families.[97]

All of the above are of particular concern to the Roma minority (commonly but inaccurately called gypsies), a previously nomadic people who nowadays still have largely transitory lifestyles and earn their livelihood from engaging in crafts, trades, and manual labor in mostly rural communities across Europe.[98] Ben Slay, Director of UNDP's Regional Centre in Bratislava notes that "[w]hile these countries grew considerably . . . the Roma's access to education, health sanitation and housing conditions does not meet most of the targets set forth by the Millennium Declaration."[99] The Roma, who constitute anywhere from 2.5 percent to 3 percent of the population in the Czech Republic to nearly 10 percent of the population of the Slovak Republic[100]are not only likely to be four to ten times as poor as the majority of the population, but they also are more likely to fall into poverty and remain there (Figure 4.1).[101]

Since the fall of the Soviet Union, native Russians, who compose just over a third of the population in Latvia and a quarter of the population in Estonia, are a minority facing frequent discrimination. Their social marginalization in these countries takes the form of restrictions on citizenship and naturalization, the inability to vote, and requirements demanding that the language of the majority is predominantly used in the school curricula.[102]

As the Central European and Baltic countries are settling into their place in the European Union, their focus is shifting more and more toward the alleviation of poverty and other social

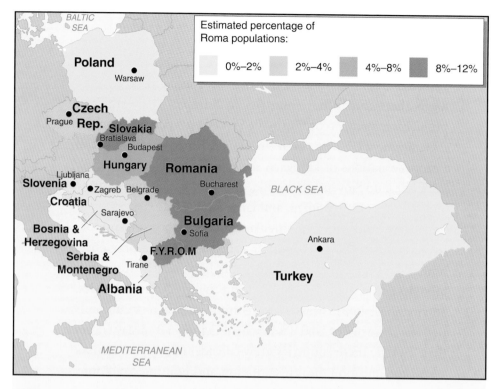

Figure 4.1 The Roma population, which comprises as high as 12 percent of the population in some Central and Eastern European countries, is one of the poorest and most discriminated-against minorities in Europe.

Source: The World Bank

development issues in order to fully comply with the standards of the EU. As their economies continue to gather steam, it is expected that these countries will fully reach the Millennium Development Goal of eradicating poverty by 2015.[103]

Southeastern Europe

The years since the collapse of communism have not been kind to the Southeastern European countries of Albania, Bosnia and Herzegovina, Bulgaria, Croatia, the former Yugoslavian Republic of Macedonia, Moldova, Romania, and Serbia and Montenegro. Starting with a severe political and economic crisis in the early 1990s, followed by the massive pyramid investment schemes that brought down the Albanian government[104] and emptied the pockets of hundreds of thousands of people across Southeastern Europe, and ending with the war in Yugoslavia and the disintegration of that state amidst ethnic cleansing and mass migrations, the period was a difficult time for the young democracies.[105]

Although relative political and economic stability has returned since the beginning of the 21st century, the legacy of over a decade of crises is still felt in the high levels of poverty and unemployment in the region and in the weakness of state institutions.[106] While the Southeastern European countries lag behind other members of the European Union in income, [107] some, such as Bulgaria and Romania, are working hard to catch up in time for their slated accession to the Union.

The poor in this part of the world usually live in the more rural areas and smaller towns farther away from the capital, and they are likely to be members of a minority group or to have less education or skills. Increasingly, they are also likely to be young and unemployed.[108] One study[109] found that today, education and labor skills have become the most significant indicators of the likelihood of someone in the region to become poor and to stay poor, because compensating for these two factors is not easily done later in life. In fact, the low education level of the breadwinner of a family makes that family four to five times more prone to poverty than a family with higher education levels.

Such rising inequalities in education levels, incomes, and standards of living are most apparent in the rural areas of Southeastern Europe. Research by the International Fund for Agricultural Development (IFAD) finds that nearly 90 percent of the poverty-stricken population of Albania lives in rural areas, while in Romania, rural poverty is twice as high as urban poverty. Furthermore, the rural population in the region is much more likely to suffer from malnutrition and disease, and to receive less or poorer quality education.[110] Not surprisingly, IFAD finds that for many rural inhabitants, agriculture is not a conscious lifestyle or career choice, but simply a self-sustainable alternative for basic food and livelihood needs.

Internally displaced people and refugees from the prolonged conflicts in the former Federal Republic of Yugoslavia represent another group of people highly vulnerable to poverty. According to the Council of Europe, in 2003 there were over 1.2 million people still unable to return to their homesteads or resume normal lives in Southeastern Europe.[111] For some of them, displacement has been a way of life for over ten years. Those who have returned have often faced resistance and discrimination, despite the international community's involvement in the process.[112] Economic depression in Bosnia and Croatia has also made it hard for the returnees to find jobs or other sustenance.

As economic growth and stability begins to return to the region, the biggest barrier to improving the plight of the poor remains the establishment of strong and transparent governing institutions in the countries of Southeastern Europe.[113] Such reliable and accountable institutions would eliminate the need for corruption, create more trade and investment opportunities, and build solid legal and regulatory foundations for the official entrance of these countries into global markets. Good governance would also improve the condition of public services in these states, which has been the main reason for the limited progress made on reaching the Millennium Development Goals, especially in the poorest countries in the region.[114]

The Commonwealth of Independent States (CIS)

During the 1990s, the rollercoaster ride experienced by Armenia, Belarus, Georgia, Moldova, Russia, and Ukraine, the six European members of the CIS, was unprecedented: the exhilaration brought by independence was followed by crushing economic shocks and deep financial crisis stemming from the currency devaluation of the Russian rouble. Many were surprised by the severity of the devastation, including the World Bank, which noted that

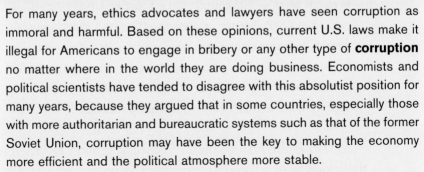

The Price of Corruption

For many years, ethics advocates and lawyers have seen corruption as immoral and harmful. Based on these opinions, current U.S. laws make it illegal for Americans to engage in bribery or any other type of **corruption** no matter where in the world they are doing business. Economists and political scientists have tended to disagree with this absolutist position for many years, because they argued that in some countries, especially those with more authoritarian and bureaucratic systems such as that of the former Soviet Union, corruption may have been the key to making the economy more efficient and the political atmosphere more stable.

More recent research, however, suggests that corruption has exactly the opposite effect. Corruption distorts the economy and endangers political stability. Today, economists see it as an arbitrary tax that unfairly harms the poor more than anybody else. Since bribes require money or other forms of wealth to pay them, those who don't have the means to pay bribes (the poor) are shut out of the system. Thus, corruption always gives advantage to the wealthy, who can pay the bribes, and to the powerful, who can demand them. Furthermore, corruption causes economic inefficiencies by favoring not the most competitive businesses, but those who are the most generous in their kickbacks. Corrupt state officials and corrupt business people both cheat the state out of legitimate tax revenues and consequently cause the state to raise taxes to compensate for the loss. Those taxes are then paid mostly by those who can't avoid them—again, the poor.

The same research study conducted surveys among the poor in four Central and Eastern European countries where corruption was still rampant in 2002: Bulgaria, the Czech Republic, Slovakia, and Ukraine. The surveys found that poor people in these countries were consistently less likely than the rich to know their rights when dealing with public officials, less satisfied in their dealings with officials, less likely to report a fair treatment, and less likely to report that they received a favorable treatment by these officials. The discrimination obvious in these results can be traced directly to the corroding effects of corruption on all levels of state institutions.

Source: Adapted from William L. Miller, "Corruption and Poverty in Postcommunist Europe," World Bank Transition Newsletter (May–June 2002): 30. Reprinted with permission.

... the decline was far more severe than expected. GDP fell on average by over 40 %, and although growth has picked up strongly in recent years, no CIS country has yet regained its pre-transition per capita GDP. Poverty increased well beyond expectations in many CIS countries, and inequality rose as well. Infant mortality fell in most of the transition countries, but life expectancy fell as well in most CIS countries. The gross enrollment rate in basic education fell in many of the transition countries.[115]

At last, at the turn of the 21st century, growth returned to the region with a bang: in 2000, the CIS posted an incredible 8.4 percent economic spur, followed by a 5.8 percent in 2001 and 4.7 percent in 2002. Central to this growth pattern has been the economy of Russia, the largest and most important export market for the rest of the CIS countries.[116] Russia's improving economic climate has sparked an increase not only in imports and industrial activity, but also in real incomes and employment,[117] sending a welcome sign that poverty indicators in the region are starting to improve.

The poor in the CIS appear to have little in common with the poor across the rest of Central and Eastern Europe. According to data collected in the last decade by the World Bank,[118] some of the commonalities include that the poor in the CIS also tend to be mostly in larger families, and, in Russia and Moldova, rural poverty is more prevalent than urban poverty. However, in Armenia and Belarus, people in urban areas are generally poorer than people in rural areas—a trend completely opposite to that of the rest of the region! Moreover, poverty among the elderly and the pensioners is less common in Belarus, Moldova, and Russia, in contrast to the situation in the rest of the countries. Another unique trend in Moldova is that women are less poor than men, while in Armenia, the inhabitants of high altitude and earthquake areas are particularly prone to high poverty.

Just as in Southeastern Europe, internally displaced persons and refugees constitute a significant subsection of the poor in the CIS (Figure 4.2). That is especially true in Azerbaijan, where the Nagorno-Karabakh conflict has resulted in 800,000 internally displaced persons (IDPs)[119] and Georgia, where ethnic disputes in Abkhazia and South Ossetia, have produced 250,000 to 300,000 IDPs.[120]

The slow and painful transition to more globalized economies and the remote geography of some of the countries in the region has been the main reason for the rather slow response to poverty alleviation. In some CIS countries, poverty remains an issue for more than half of their populations.[121]

Most of the CIS countries have adopted the Poverty Reduction Strategy Paper (PRSP) approach recommended by the inter-governmental organizations (IGOs) as a first step toward the eradication of poverty. Although their strategies may vary from country to country, most PRSPs focus first on the need to recognize and monitor poverty in the region in all its forms (both monetary and non-monetary) and second on the daunting task of designing the major reforms needed at all levels of the state (governmental, social, fiscal, political, and so on) to allow for the economic growth and opportunity needed to eradicate poverty.[122]

CURRENT TRENDS

Overall, the developing countries in Central and Eastern Europe seem to have left the hardest stages of transition behind them. Nevertheless, many of them are still struggling to cope with the remaining issues of high poverty, high unemployment, poor public services, and limited opportunities for their people. It is clear that for many states, the goal of inclusion in the European Union (EU) has served and is serving as a motivating factor to continue on the path to globalization, despite the personal and societal hardships associated with the transition. The success of countries like Poland, the Czech Republic, and Hungary is yet another proof that democratic, open-market societies are better equipped to deal with social ills such as poverty.

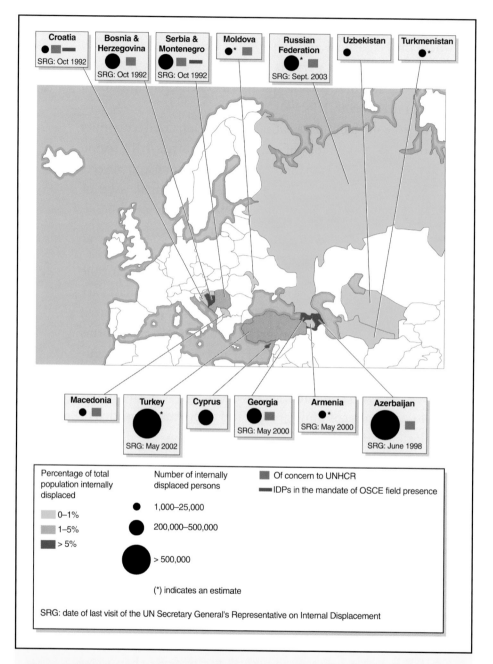

Figure 4.2 The many internally displaced people in some European and Central Asian countries are also some of the poorest in the region.

Source: The Global IDP (Internally Displaced Persons) Project

Poverty in Latin America and the Caribbean

What would cause more than half the people on an entire continent to embrace democracy and then denounce it within a couple of decades? Why would nearly 300 million people declare that they are ready to give up their freedom? In Latin America, the reason is the faint hope that that would give them a chance to get out of poverty. A recent extensive poll conducted in 18 Latin American countries and including hundreds of current and former heads of state and other national leaders indicates that a deep crisis of confidence in the democratic system is permeating the region, mainly as a result of the pervasive poverty and economic disparities and the inability of governments to do anything about them.[123]

The startling results—that many Latin Americans would choose to live in authoritarian regimes if that ensured them a better income and job opportunities—prompted the UN Secretary-General Kofi Annan to say: "That is very sad. More important, it is wrong. The solution to Latin America's ills does not lie in a return to authoritarianism. It lies in a stronger and deeper-rooted democracy."[124]

To fully understand how poverty and instability caused a major world region to question the very foundation of a free and modern society, one has to look at the globalization efforts of the last two decades and the current social, economic and political situation of the Latin American and Caribbean (LAC) region.

RECENT GLOBALIZATION EFFORTS

Since the 1980s, the LAC region embarked on the path to democratization and modernization of its economy that, while successful in accomplishing the former, failed miserably on the latter objective. Most of the countries in the region became democratic during that decade, but were unable to translate these beneficial political reforms into an economic success, giving the period the infamous name of "the lost decade."[125] During those years, the region experienced a sharp decline in economic growth rates, a sharp increase in inflation rates, and a crushing foreign debt from which it has still to recover.[126]

In the 1990s, the LAC region continued its globalization efforts via widespread market liberalization reforms, multilateral trade agreements, and monetary policy adjustments, as prescribed by organizations such as the International Monetary Fund (IMF) and the World Bank. Again, the end results were uneven at best. Many countries were able to take control over inflation, make their foreign debt more manageable and attract foreign investment in the region, but they were unable to increase economic growth, create more jobs, or reduce poverty and inequality in any significant way.[127]

The Latin Americans of the generation that grew up during the last two decades of the 20th century have known only economic chaos and social strife in their lives, and their patience with the status quo is running out. [128]

CURRENT PERSPECTIVES

While the current economic situation in most LAC countries has stabilized after the global economic downturn and the 9/11-related crisis, the human and social development in the region remains persistently inadequate.[129] Nearly half of the population in the region (4 percent) still lives on less than $2 a day in 2003, compared with 41 percent in 1980 (Figure 5.1).[130] The UN itself admits that although 11 of the 18 countries studied for its *Democracy in Latin America* report showed a decrease in poverty, and in 15 of them the per capita income grew between 1991 and 2002, in all but 3 countries over a quarter of the population remains poor.[131]

Simply put, democratic reforms have not resulted in widespread economic progress, despite the best hopes and efforts of some politicians and economists. The reasons for this startling effect, particular to the LAC region, range from inequality and corruption to poor education and protectionism. We will examine these factors in more detail in the following sections.

Inequality

The LAC region has the highest level of unequal income distribution in the world. The most affluent 10 percent of all Latin Americans earn almost half of all the income in the region (48 percent), while the most destitute 10 percent earn only 1.6 percent of the region's income.[132] In some countries, this stark disparity is even more apparent. For example, in the Central American countries of Guatemala and Honduras, the richest 20 percent of the population receive 60 percent of the income, while the bottom 40 percent gets merely 10 percent of the income.[133]

Even the relatively healthy economic growth rate of the last few years has not been able to narrow that disparity. The reason is that the aggregate growth rate has gone up mainly due to economic activity in only a few isolated areas and industries, thus benefiting only the limited number of local workers and not filtering down to the majority of the population. A case in point

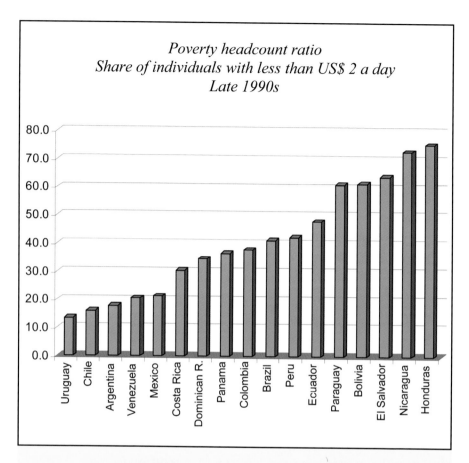

Poverty headcount ratio
Share of individuals with less than US$ 2 a day
Late 1990s

Figure 5.1 Poverty levels in Latin America and the Caribbean remain very high despite some recent positive developments.

Source: Leonardo Gasparini, "Different Lives: Inequality in Latin America and the Caribbean," World Bank LAC Flagship Report, July 29, 2003, p. 114.

is Peru, where, since 2001, the economy has been growing at close to 4 percent annually, but the majority of people have not seen the benefits.[134] This dissonant effect has prompted Alejandro Toledo, the president of Peru, to say: "What good is an impressive growth rate? Wall Street applauds us, but in the streets, no. So what good is it?"[135]

The frustration of politicians and citizens alike is not enough to erase the effects of centuries of inequalities entrenched in the region.]Ever since the era of European colonization, the continent's native people have served as the enslaved and exploited labor force for the predominantly white ruling class. Today, this heritage of class and ethnic differences is echoed in unequal access to education and other services, as well as earnings potential.[136] When other factors such as the higher number of children in poor households and the limited access of the poor to public services are factored in, it becomes clear why inequality is such a stubborn phenomenon in the LAC region.[137]

It is not surprising then, to find that, according to one poll, 71 percent of Latin Americans believe that their countries are "governed for the benefit of a few powerful interests" and not for "the good of everyone."[138] Such distrust and dissatisfaction is unlikely to disappear until the situation improves. The good news is that even small improvements may yield large results. A joint report by several organizations on the status of the Millennium Development Goals in LAC finds that even a tiny reduction in inequality can result in a high rate of poverty reduction in the region.[139]

Corruption and Political Instability

Recently, an angry mob in the small town of Ilave, Peru, beat to death the town's mayor and badly injured four of his councilmen because they believed them to be corrupt and inefficient.[140] Although an extreme example of the resentment and mistrust permeating Latin American societies, this incident is only one in a long string of politically charged crises: six elected state leaders were ousted in the space of a few years[141]; Peruvian president Toledo's ratings are down to 8 percent due to allegations of corruption[142]; 70 percent of Mexicans do not trust their government representatives[143]; and 59 percent of all LAC politicians agree that their parties are failing at their job.[144]

Maybe even more disturbing is the fact that the legal and social institutions, traditionally seen as the ultimate protectors of the poor and the disadvantaged, are not faring any better. The deep disillusionment with democracy in LAC is partially due to the failure of the courts and social service networks in the region to operate without crippling rates of corruption, nepotism, and bias.[145]

The negative effect of these social ills is felt also in the business sector, which is mainly responsible for the creation of new and better paying jobs in the region. According to the report *Doing Business in 2005* recently issued by the World Bank, four Latin American countries Ecuador, Guatemala, Honduras, and Venezuela were among the nations with the worst business climate, while collectively, Latin America was the region with the worst legal protection for financial transactions and the least efficient system for the resolution of business issues.[146] The report does rank Colombia as the second most improved country for business, due to its efforts to improve the climate for investors and new business registrations.[147]

The United Nations Development Programme (UNDP) rightly points out that "[b]uilding a new legitimacy for the state" must be a key action area for the region, if it wants to get back on the track of economic growth and poverty reduction. [148] In its *Human Development Report 2002*, the organization's administrator, Mark Malloch Brown, draws an even more direct link between political stability and poverty elimination: "Sustained poverty reduction requires equitable growth—but also requires that poor people have political power. And the best way to achieve that in a manner consistent with human development objectives is by building strong and deep forms of democratic governance at all levels of society." [149]

Ethnic tensions

There is a decidedly ethnic aspect of poverty in Latin America and the Caribbean. Statistics show that in Mexico, for example, 81 percent of the indigenous people live below the poverty line, while the same can be said for only 18 percent of the rest of the population.[150] Eighty percent of Ecuador's native and African-Ecuadorian population also lives in poverty,[151] while in Bolivia, Brazil, Guatemala and Peru, the poor are twice as likely to be indigenous or descendants of Africans as the general population.[152]

These numbers speak volumes against the region's self-proclaimed color-blindness, which is discussed at length in Amy Chua's book *World on Fire: How Exporting Free Market Democracy Breeds Ethnic Hatred and Global Instability.*[153] In a chapter dedicated to Latin America, the author talks about how since the colonial era, the "pigmentocracy" phenomenon has continued to segregate and discriminate against people who possess the physical characteristics of the native population, such as darker skin and hair, and shorter height.[154] In only three Latin American countries—Argentina, Uruguay, and Chile, is this issue not apparent, mainly because their indigenous populations were nearly wiped out centuries ago during the age of the conquistadors (Figure 5.2).[155] Thanks to globalization, however, after centuries of internalizing a deep sense of worthlessness, many of the indigenous people are starting to see their heritage as a source of pride, according to Chua. Through now widely available media and communication sources, native peoples are learning from their leaders to be proud of their heritage and fight for their rights.[156] Increasingly, the message is translated into disruptive and even violent uprisings, most recently in Peru, Ecuador, and Bolivia.[157] The most common demands of the indigenous people continue to be for more economic opportunity, equality, political representation, and poverty reduction assistance.

Troubled Economies

The economic chaos of the last two decades in Latin America has resulted not only in the public's distrust in the democratic system and intergovernmental organizations such as the World Bank, but also in large unemployment rates and in the growth of an informal economy that is the second-largest in the world. The **informal economy**, also called the black market, a term that

Figure 5.2 The indigenous, or native, people of Latin America suffer the most from poverty and discrimination. These two Guambianos Indians plow the land near the village of Guambia, Cauca Province, in this photograph taken in 2001. The living conditions of Colombia's indigenous people, a population of about 1 million out of about a total population of 40 million, are the worst in Latin America.

describes economic activity that happens outside the legal and fiscal systems of states, includes such occupations as unlicensed street vendors, home-based workers working "under the table," seasonal or temporary workers who are not "on the books," and other similar jobs.[158]

In Latin America and the Caribbean, the informal economy accounted for (on average) over 41 percent of the gross national product (GNP) in 2003 (Figure 5.3).[159] What's more, according to the International Labor Organization, nearly half of all jobs in the LAC region are in the informal economy and two-thirds of all new jobs also originate there.[160]

The consequences for both the citizens and the countries are dire. Working in low-paying, informal economy jobs not only

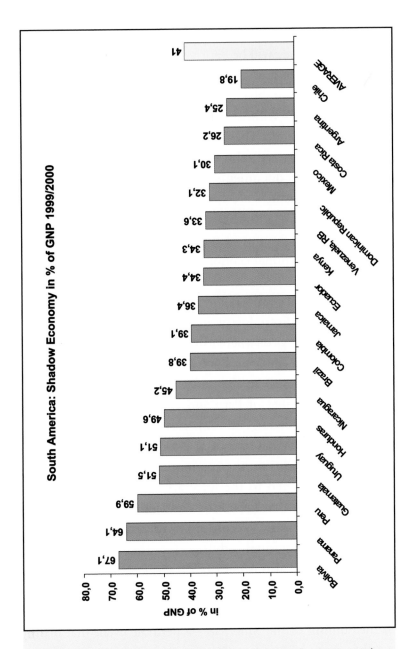

South America: Shadow Economy in % of GNP 1999/2000

Country	% of GNP
AVERAGE	41
Chile	19,8
Argentina	25,4
Costa Rica	26,2
Mexico	30,1
Dominican Republic	32,1
Venezuela, RB	33,6
Kenya	34,3
Ecuador	34,4
Jamaica	36,4
Colombia	39,1
Brazil	39,8
Nicaragua	45,2
Honduras	49,6
Uruguay	51,1
Guatemala	51,5
Peru	59,9
Panama	64,1
Bolivia	67,1

Figure 5.3 South America's "shadow economy" represented a large percentage of the Gross National Product for 1999/2000 and contributes to the persistent poverty in the region.

Source: Friedrich Schneider, *Size and Measurement of the Informal Economy in 110 Countries Around the World*, World Bank report, 2002, p.12.

isn't enough to get families out of poverty, it also is a virtual guarantee that they will be deprived of benefits such as insurance, medical care, and savings.[161] Furthermore, because they are working on the black market, these people are limited to doing business with only a few trusted family members, neighbors, or friends. They are shut out from banks or other lenders, and they are reluctant to apply for legal licenses, utilities, or proper documents because the processes for establishing a legal business are costly and slow.[162] This reluctance in turn affects the state's ability to collect taxes and to account for the economic output of underground businesses, further paralyzing the national economy and keeping the unemployment rate high.

Even when legal employment can be found, it usually requires low skills and delivers low wages. From the *maquiladoras* of Honduras and Mexico (where usually U.S. suppliers hire mostly local women to assemble products that are then re-exported back to the United States) to the coffee fields of Costa Rica and Nicaragua, the mines of Peru and Chile and the oil fields of Venezuela and Ecuador, Latin Americans are toiling in agriculture and industries that have been associated with perpetuating poverty.[163] In addition, the economic effect of these industries is often limited to the local area. "These are generally enclave activities that have little connection with the rest of the national economy," according to Ricardo Ffrench-Davis, the principal regional advisor for the UN Economic Commission on Latin America.[164]

Poor Education

At the Summit of the Americas—a periodic event that brings together many leaders from Western Hemisphere countries to discuss current regional issues—in Quebec City in 2001, all participating countries declared in a joint staement: "Education is the key to strengthening democratic institutions, promoting the development of human potential, equality and understanding among our peoples, as well as sustaining economic growth and reducing poverty." A goal was set to ensure that at least 75 percent of all children will have access to secondary education by 2010.[165]

Only few years later, however, it has become apparent that the LAC region will not be able to achieve this goal in time and will continue to lag behind other world regions. Although most LAC countries have around 90 percent enrollment in primary education, it is unlikely that most of them will reach 75 percent enrollment in secondary education.[166] Not surprisingly, the majority of the students missing from the high school classrooms will be from poor and indigenous households.[167]

What's more, the quality of the education in Latin America is below par. For example, the Program for International Student Assessment (PISA) discovered that in Mexico, Chile, Peru, Argentina, and Brazil, 16 percent to 24 percent of the 15 year olds who have learned basic reading skills are unable to translate the materials they read into meaningful knowledge.[168] The poor educational quality is blamed on several different factors, including unqualified teachers, poorly organized education systems, and a lack of clearly set standards for performance.[169]

More importantly, such poor education or lack of education can be linked to low labor wages and poverty. Researchers have found that countries with poor education ratings usually have more low-paid workers than countries with better education systems.[170] They further conclude that better education is likely to result in higher productivity and earnings and therefore, lower poverty levels.[171]

Gender Differences

The topic of poverty in LAC countries would not be complete without discussing the differences in poverty levels between the genders. In a region where close to one-third of all households are headed by a woman, the deficiency of programs for poverty alleviation designed specifically for women is troubling, according to the UN.[172]

Women usually face more and different obstacles to obtaining a job, ranging from cultural stereotypes against women working outside the home to a lack of vocational training, child-care options, and access to information about available jobs. Less than half of all working-age women in the LAC region have jobs, and even when they do, women usually devote a larger portion of their pay to their children's needs, in the hope of providing them with the chance to escape poverty.[173]

Some of the basic measurements of progress in women's rights are access to reproductive health services and public policies empowering women. In that aspect, Latin America's progress in advancing this agenda is on par with that of the rest of the developing countries. However, the overall numbers for the region do not account for the large differences among the countries. For example, while Costa Rica, Cuba, and Chile have reduced their infant mortality rate to no more than 12 per 1,000 births—a rate close to that of developed countries—in Bolivia, the number jumps almost fivefold to 56 per 1,000 and in Haiti, it is 63 per 1,000.[174]

BUILDING ON THE POSITIVE TRENDS FOR THE FUTURE

Although much remains to be done before Latin America can claim success in the fight against poverty and inequality, the region needs only to look to the progress made in some of the countries to find hope. For example, Mexico has seen much-needed improvements in poverty reduction in the new century, achieved through growth in unskilled labor income, balancing the urban-rural income levels, and a commitment to government-sponsored programs such as Oportunidades, which provides aid to poor families to improve their nutrition and keep their children healthy and in school.[175]

To break out of the seemingly vicious circle of economic underperformance and poverty, Latin American countries can also look to Chile as a role model in implementing successful market reforms, according to Ian Vásquez of the CATO Institute. Chile, which ranks 22nd on the *Economic Freedom of the World: 2004 Annual Report* published by the CATO Institute, has been able to grow economically and cut poverty in half while remaining stable and democratic.[176] To replicate this success in other countries, Vásquez states, Latin America should focus on eliminating bureaucracy, lowering taxes, and building stronger legal defenses for property rights.

To gain better leverage against the sometimes protectionist trade policies of developed countries, Latin American states also should continue forming regional economic alliances, such as MERCOSUR, which encompasses Argentina, Brazil, Uruguay, and Paraguay, and the Andean Community, formed by Venezuela, Colombia, Bolivia, Ecuador and Peru.[177]

The future is looking bright for the LAC regions, according to many economists, who are impressed with the success of countries like Chile, Brazil, and Peru to attract investment, control inflation, and reduce spending, and by Uruguay and Argentina, which have made great strides forward since the crises of 2001–2002.[178]

In 2002, the UNDP and other organizations published *Meeting the Millennium Poverty Reduction Targets in Latin America and the Caribbean*, a report that looks at the conditions under which 18 LAC countries would be able to meet the extreme poverty reduction target established as one of the United Nations Millennium Development Goals. According to the report, if Latin American countries attain economic success and distribute it more equally among its populations, the changes needed to ensure that each one of the nations reaches the Millennium Development Goals are within reach.[179]

Poverty in the
Developed Countries

Poverty has been a condition of human existence. It has shifted and evolved together with our civilization and has assumed many different forms over the ages, according to the level of cultural, social, political, and economic development of each society. To this day, almost all societies continue to grapple with poverty, including the wealthiest and most advanced ones—those termed developed or industrialized nations.

THE MEANING OF POVERTY IN DEVELOPED COUNTRIES
As discussed in the first chapter of this book, economists, sociologists, and other researchers often use different measures for poverty. Some prefer the monetary approach, where poverty is evaluated strictly in terms of an absolute minimum income level that separates the poor

from the non-poor, usually a $1 a day or $2 a day standard favored by the World Bank, the International Monetary Fund, and other world organizations. Others prefer more relative and multidimensional measures that take into consideration social indicators such as access to medical care, safe water, and education, that distinguish the poor from the non-poor.

When it comes to the developed countries, it is clear that a strictly monetary approach would be not only inappropriate, given the much higher levels of income, but also misleading. Considering that per capita gross domestic product (GDP) in G7, the group of seven major industrialized countries (consisting of Canada, France, Germany, Italy, Japan, United Kingdom, and the United States) for 2004 was over $31,000,[180] no one who lives in these countries would fall under the $1 or $2 a day standards. That does not mean however, that poverty doesn't exist in those and other developed countries; it means that it has to be defined by a different set of economic and social indicators.

One alternative is to measure levels of poverty not by an across-the-board, global baseline, but by the economic potential of each society. Thus, a widely accepted standard for measuring poverty in developed nations is to consider someone poor who is not able

Purchasing Power Parity

It is not so simple to compare incomes from country to country, because fluctuating exchange rates mean that what a U.S. dollar will buy in, say, Indonesia may vary from day to day. Therefore, analysts use **purchasing power parity dollars (PPP)**, units that reflect what it costs to buy a common bundle of goods and services, expressed in some common currency, usually U.S. dollars. To say that someone in Kenya has $3,000 in PPP units means that he or she can buy in Kenya the equivalent of what could be purchased with 3,000 U.S. dollars in the United States.

Source: Stephen R. Shalom, *Which Side Are You On? An Introduction to Politics* (Boston: Longman, 2003), 328. Copyright © 2003. Reprinted by permission of Pearson Education, Inc.

to reach an income level equal to half of the national median income. In some cases, this threshold can fluctuate to as high as 60 percent of the national per capita income and in others, to as low as 40 percent, but the overall trend is to divide the poor from the non-poor at the 50 percent threshold.[181] Such relative measure is flexible enough to account for the typical fluctuations in economic cycles and to always show poverty levels in relation to the overall economic situation in a country. It also lends itself to cross-country comparisons.

Another important consideration is how the income is distributed among the population as a whole. National averages tend to smooth over the inequalities in the earnings across social classes and political systems, for example. A country that has a high per capita GDP may have arrived at that number by averaging the very high income of a small portion of the population with the relatively low income of a large part of the population. This may result in an overall impressive measure of well being for the country, but also in a bleak rate of poverty for those at the bottom of the income pyramid. Conversely, if a country manages to keep the incomes of all members of society more or less equal, the poverty rate there will be minimal.[182]

Poverty in developed countries can be also defined in terms of lack of resources other than income. Some studies measure the availability of necessities, such as food and shelter,[183] while others assess abilities such as education and work skills.[184] In more recent years, the concept of social exclusion has been linked with poverty and is used as a measure of it in some regions.[185] (Differences in national and regional approaches to poverty measurement and management methods will be discussed later in this chapter.)

It is also important to note that income poverty in the industrialized world is usually a transitory condition. Many people may slip into poverty for only a few months and then get out of it, while others remain poor for extended periods of time or experience poverty on a recurring basis. Suffice it to say that poverty is not a static condition, despite what the statistics may suggest. Researchers estimated that at any point during a year, between 6 percent and 20 percent of the populations of Canada, Germany, the Netherlands, and Sweden have incomes below the poverty threshold, but that in fact only 1 percent to 2 percent of those people stay poor.[186] Data from the United States paints a similar picture. Over half of the "poverty spells" lasted for four months or less, and nearly 80 percent of them lasted less than a year, with only 2 percent of the poor experiencing continuous poverty for the full four-year study period.[187]

WHO ARE THE POOR IN DEVELOPED COUNTRIES?

Much of the recent research on poverty in developed countries is based on a large and ongoing project called the Luxembourg Income Study. This cooperative project, started in 1983, tracks over 130 indicators of income and economic well being in 29 industrialized nations via household income surveys and labor force surveys that then allow scientists and policy makers to analyze trends, formulate strategies, and evaluate the effects of certain economic, political, or social frameworks.[188]

Based on this data, researchers have found that, despite century-old efforts to eliminate it, poverty has actually increased in the last two decades in developed countries, regardless of the differences in their welfare systems.[189] The social groups most at risk of being poor are usually the young, the unemployed, women, and ethnic minorities.

Children

Poverty among children is a central concern in all nations, but its presence in developed nations is particularly troubling. Although many social policies and programs have been specifically designed to alleviate it, none has accomplished its goal.

Besides the innate need to help the most helpless and innocent members of society, the war on childhood poverty is fueled by more practical concerns: children growing without the threat and disadvantages of poverty are more likely to avoid it in adulthood, and thus become a fully contributing members of the society. The ripple effects pay off not only by reducing society's burden to carry for the poor, but also in countless other social, fiscal, economic, and personal benefits. Since poverty tends to be perpetuated through the family situation, the advantages of alleviating it early in a person's life can be sustained for future generations.[190]

Unfortunately, many developed countries have a long way to go before reaching that goal. This is especially true for English-speaking countries such as the United States, Canada, Australia, New Zealand, the United Kingdom, and Ireland, where childhood poverty is substantially higher than in continental Europe. The highest number of children considered poor is in the United States, where nearly one-quarter of all children live in low-income households (Figure 6.1).[191] Financial poverty, however, is only one part of the story. The English-speaking countries also score high on other poverty indicators such as teenage pregnancies, which triple the rate of that of European teenagers.[192]

In education, the differences are not so stark. Although international comparisons of education systems are relative at best, the fact that in all countries of the G8 group (consisting of the G7 countries plus Russia) at least 13 percent of young people have not completed secondary education shows that work remains to be done. The United States shows the highest level of high school graduates at 87 percent, followed by Germany and Japan at 81percent, Canada at 79 percent, the U.K. and France at 62 percent, and Italy at 42 percent.[193]

Perhaps more telling is the effect that completing or not completing secondary education has on earnings later in life. In the United States, those who did not graduate high school earned on average 33 percent less than high school graduates, while in France the difference was 16 percent; in Canada, 17 percent; and in Germany, 22 percent.[194] The large difference

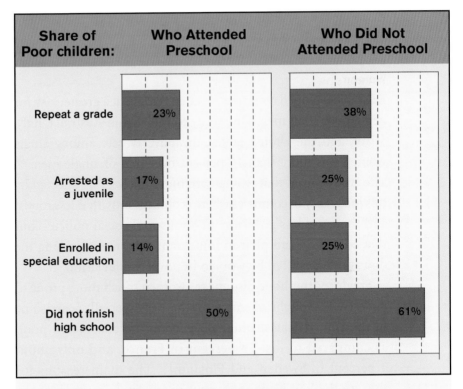

Share of Poor children:	Who Attended Preschool	Who Did Not Attended Preschool
Repeat a grade	23%	38%
Arrested as a juvenile	17%	25%
Enrolled in special education	14%	25%
Did not finish high school	50%	61%

Figure 6.1 A significant percentage of children in the United States who cannot attend preschool because of poverty remain disadvantaged throughout their school years.

Source: University of Wisconsin

in earnings between graduates and non-graduates in the United States is consistent with the country's high inequality and high poverty rates.

Finally, it is both disheartening and encouraging to know that it could cost governments very little to help most children out of poverty, because so many of them live in households just below the relative poverty line. It is disheartening, because nothing has been done about it yet, and encouraging because it seems to be a fairly easy thing to do. The United Nations Children's Fund (UNICEF) has determined that in two of the most developed countries with two of the highest poverty rates for children—the United States and the United Kingdom—

it would take spending just over 0.5 percent of the GNP to alleviate childhood poverty altogether.[195]

Women

Even in developed countries, women remain at a greater risk for being poor than men. One study found that in Australia, Italy, Spain, and the United States, the poverty rate among single women was more than 10 percent over that of single men.[196] The study found that women are more likely to be affected by this inequality in countries where economic growth is less robust and there are less government-sponsored social policies, but that education can play an important role in eliminating the disadvantages faced by women in poverty alleviation.[197]

Single motherhood also makes women much more prone to poverty. The plight of single mothers is especially worrisome in the United States, where 45 percent are considered poor, as compared to just 13 percent in France, and only about 5 percent in Sweden and Finland.[198] The main reasons for this are the low-paying jobs that many single mothers in the United States are likely to work in and the lack of strong social benefits, such as government-sponsored child-care and health care, geared towards working mothers.[199] Other factors, such as the lower education level attained by many single mothers, also prevents them from earning better incomes. Lastly, mothers are less likely to have a successful career because they have to spend time away from the office more often for their childrearing duties, and they often receive less than adequate child support from the fathers of their children.[200]

In many European countries, the social benefits are also considered inadequate in regard to single parents (who are usually women). One study recommends that more social assistance policies should be designed with single mothers or women in mind.[201] In several developed countries, notably Australia, Canada, Germany, and Sweden, however, the poverty rate for single-parent households has decreased significantly in the last decade.[202]

Unemployed

"Joblessness is the main cause of poverty," unequivocally states a recent study from the Organization for Economic Co-operation and Development (OECD).[203] Many other studies agree. While joblessness is a much less frequent phenomenon in the developed world, its experience leads to a similar result—poverty— as in developing countries. What is different are the dynamics of it.

Across industrialized societies, an unusual process called "employment polarization" has been taking place in the last decade. The number of households with all adults working has been rising, as has the number of households in which no adults are working, but the number of households with only one adult working has been on the decline. This divergence has played a significant role in the relationship between poverty and employment. While the rates of poor households who have two or more income-generating adults have remained almost negligible, households with no working adults have experienced growing rates of poverty. The trend is especially high in Canada, Germany, Ireland and the United States, where 40 percent of workless households are poor.[204]

According to the U.S. Census Bureau, the unemployed were over three times as likely to be poor than full-time workers. Furthermore, although nearly 40 percent of those experiencing poverty were employed, only about 11 percent of them held a full-time position, while 26 percent of them worked only part-time.[205]

An exception to the solid connection between unemployment and poverty is the case of Scandinavian countries, where poverty is rarely a direct consequence of unemployment. The reasons for this unique situation are the comprehensive social welfare systems of these countries and their more even distributions of income.[206] The smaller size of these countries also plays a role, as does the predominance of households with two income earners—a full 87 percent of households in Finland and Sweden, for example.[207]

It is encouraging that other developed countries are following the example of the Scandinavian countries when it comes
to unemployment benefits structure. Australia, Austria,
Belgium, Finland, Ireland, and the United Kingdom have all
adopted a more "progressive" benefits distribution pattern,
while Canada, Norway, Sweden and Denmark are increasingly
using welfare benefits to protect the middle class from sliding
into poverty because of unemployment.[208]

Ethnic minorities and immigrants

Throughout the developed countries, one's ethnic background or
country of origin can influence his or her chances of being poor
(Figure 6.2). In the European Union, migrant workers, who
have supplemented the native labor force for years (especially in
low-paying jobs), are more likely to be poor than the general population. The most current research shows that some foreigners—
particularly the young, the very old, and women—are most
vulnerable. This is the case for immigrants from countries outside
Europe, who are not only most likely to hold the lowest paying
jobs, but whose unemployment is also at least 5 percent higher
than that of any other workers. They are also much more often
victims of discrimination, exploitation and social exclusion.[209]

In 2002 data, African-American and Hispanics minorities in
the United States also had a higher incidence of poverty than
whites: 24 percent and 22 percent versus 8 percent, respectively,
while people of Asian descent maintained a 10 percent poverty
rate.[210] Only Native Americans have experienced relative progress
in the fight against poverty, with a 27 percent increase in their
per capita income in the last decade of the 20th century
and an 80 percent rise in post-secondary school enrollment.
Nevertheless, Native Americans, especially those who still live
on reservations, continue to suffer higher poverty and higher
unemployment rates than the general U.S. population.[211]

The foreign born in the United States have a rate of poverty
that is, at over 16 percent, double that of the white population.

Figure 6.2 Many of the poor in developed countries are from the minority population or recent immigrants. The mother of this large Hispanic family living in Oregon receives welfare in a new program whereby she needs to work at a local hospital to keep benefits.

Interestingly, naturalized citizens were 50 percent less likely to be poor than those foreign born who have not become citizens. Furthermore, while the number of poor immigrants grew in the last few years, the overall poverty rate remained the same for them, while both the number and the poverty rate of the general population grew.[212]

POVERTY ALLEVIATION PROGRAMS
IN THE DEVELOPED COUNTRIES

The **welfare state** is a social system in which it is assumed that the government has the primary responsibility for the welfare of its citizens. Based on the democratic principles of fairness and equal opportunity, the welfare systems in developed countries are expressions of the public's concern for the disadvantaged. Currently, welfare states and their policies are continuing to evolve and adapt to keep pace with globalization and other worldwide phenomena associated with it.

History of the Welfare System

In his classic book *The Wealth of Nations* (1776), economist Adam Smith describes poverty as the lack of "necessaries," which he considers "not only the commodities which are necessary for the support of life, but whatever the custom of the country renders it indecent for creditable people, even of the lowest order, to be without."[213] The notion that all citizens of a country should be able to live at some minimum and widely accepted standard is a founding principle of the welfare system.

In the late 19th century, the German Chancellor Otto von Bismarck, for largely political reasons, was the first head of state to implement a social security system. Threatened by the powerful labor movements at the time, the other European states soon followed and, by the time World War I broke out, most European states had instituted one form or another of a social protection system.[213]

As modern society evolved, many governments added more and more programs, resulting in the comprehensive suite of state-sponsored benefits that people in most industrialized nations enjoy today including social security, unemployment insurance, disability insurance, forms of health insurance, public education, child care, maternity benefits, minimum wage and other workplace regulations, and many programs supporting the poor, such as food stamps, Medicaid, and child supplements.[215]

Despite their common philosophy, some substantial differences exist among the social policies of the developed countries, especially between the welfare systems of the European countries and that of the United States. Many of the differences can be explained by the dissimilar attitudes in these countries towards poverty.

Welfare Systems in the Industrialized World

When comparing basic beliefs about the poor, the authors of the recently published book *Fighting Poverty in the U.S. and Europe,* found out that twice as many Europeans as Americans believe that people get trapped in poverty. What's more, on the question of whether poor people are generally lazy, a full 60 percent of Americans answered "yes" compared to only 24 percent of Europeans. Lastly, while only 30 percent of Americans believed that luck plays a big role in determining income, over half (54 percent) of Europeans did.[216]

These differing attitudes shed light on the way poverty is measured on both sides of the Atlantic. European studies of poverty regularly assume a higher threshold, usually 60 percent of median income, and increasingly measure social exclusion as another indicator of poverty,[217] while in the United States, 50 percent of median income is considered the threshold and poverty is measured mainly in monetary terms.[218]

Accordingly, Europe is much more likely to provide assistance to the poor through government means and state-wide institutions, while the United States relies more on private donations, charities, foundations, and other non-governmental institutions. The manner in which governments or society redistributes resources from the better off to the poor has a lot to do with history, cultural characteristics, religion, geography, and politics.

The European welfare states are deeply influenced by the strength of post-WWII labor unions and social democratic parties, which became more committed to social equality and strong state institutions than the more conservative political systems of the United States and Britain, for example.[219]

Consequently, the generous welfare programs in Europe and especially in the Scandinavian countries typically include government-subsidized health care, month-long paid vacations every year, extended paid maternity or paternity leaves for new parents, generous pensions for retirees, and other public entitlements often unheard of in the United States.

Some equalizing factors do reduce this seemingly large disparity in welfare benefits between United States and European nations. First, a comparison between the cash and non-cash benefits among the developed countries shows that the U.S.

government spends more on health care and education for its citizens, which raises its level of non-cash transfers (Figure 6.3). Second, the European states tax their citizens and welfare recipients at a much higher overall rate, thus lowering the net benefits received by the needy.[220]

In sum, the general differences among welfare systems remain: European, and particularly Scandinavian countries, spend the most on welfare for their citizens, while English-speaking nations spend the least, at least on cash benefits.[221] These findings are consistent with the overall poverty rates in developed countries, but they hide the deeper differences among the countries, such as attitudes towards the poor, the socially more progressive thinking of Europe as opposed to the more conservative systems of the Anglo-Saxon countries, and the reliance on more government transfers in Europe versus the reliance on more private and non-governmental charity in English-speaking nations.

GLOBALIZATION AND THE WELFARE STATES

How are the poor in developed countries affected by globalization? Is the generous welfare system a viable option for the future? How is the example of the industrialized nations followed in other newly globalized countries?

The age of globalization has not had much effect on poverty rates, which for the most part have remained stable in developed countries. However, the composition of the poor has changed substantially because of globalization. Today, ethnic and racial minorities and immigrant populations constitute large parts of the poor in the wealthy Western world, as do the young and single mothers (Figure 6.4).

The elderly, which also rely heavily on government benefits, represent a growing portion of the population in developed countries and are expected to collectively cause a surge in welfare spending in the near future. In fact, the increased spending on social security benefits for the aging population of the West is one of the main reasons why poverty rates have not gone down

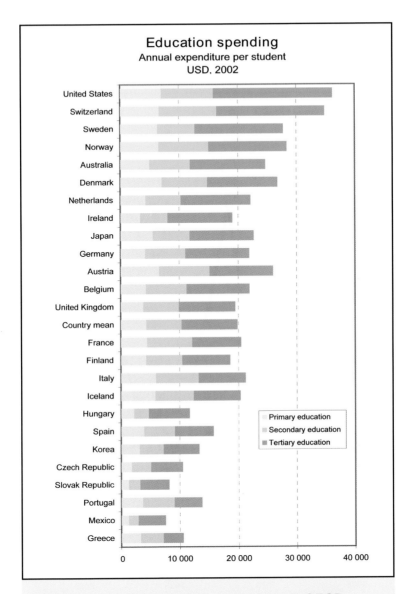

Figure 6.3 Annual Expenditure per student in OECD (Organisation for Economic Co-operation and Development) countries in USD (U.S. dollars), 2002. The United States leads in overall spending per student based on its spending for tertiary education, while Denmark spends the most on primary school students and Switzerland leads in spending per secondary school students.

Source: Organisation for Economic Co-operation and Development

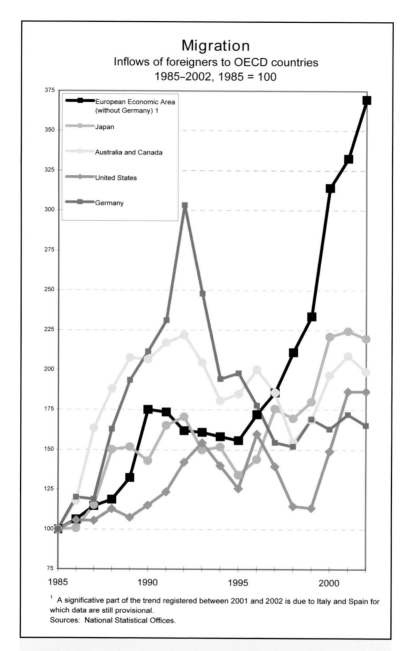

Figure 6.4 Migration-inflows of foreigners to OECD countries, 1985–2000. Immigration increased substantially in Europe since the creation of an integrated labor market.

Source: Organisation for Economic Co-operation and Development

for the other segments of the population.[222] One hypothesis maintains that because of the increased pressures on competition, labor markets, and economic efficiency, globalization will eventually dismantle welfare systems in the developed world and prevent them from forming at all in developing countries. However, some preliminary studies done by the Watson Institute indicate that just the opposite may be true—more international trade and networks may allow governments to spend more on public benefits.[223]

How poverty alleviation programs in the richer nations will evolve in response to global changes remains to be seen, but one thing is clear: economic prosperity coupled with social responsibility among citizens and fairly redistributed by governments in the form of cash or non-cash benefits has been a successful recipe for poverty reduction (as compared to developing world standards) in the developed countries. So much so that even talking about poverty there seems outrageous to some from more disadvantaged nations, such as this Papua-New Guinea native, currently studying in Australia who wrote in response to an article about poor children in the West:

> What poverty?? Real poverty is when you struggle to feed and provide for your siblings. Its when the closest health facility is a few days walk away, its when the only form of clothing your child owns is a rag taken from an old . . . sack. Real poverty should not be allowed to exist. If only the "haves" could stretch out to those around them in their community, locally first then country-wide then worldwide, instead of been so greedy and engrossed in their own materialistic cocoons we could help stamp out poverty.
>
> —Momia Teariki-Tautea, FRACP trainee
> (registrar) Princess Margaret Hospital
> for Children, WA, Australia

Current Global Initiatives for Eradicating Poverty

Poverty alleviation has, in one way or another, become a part of the strategic agendas for all players in the globalization arena today. Whether it is an explicit organizational goal, as it is for the inter-governmental organizations; a response to their perceived mis-management and bias, as in the case of anti-globalization groups; a matter of national policy, as it is for many developed countries; a good business practice, as in the case of multinational companies (MNCs); or a matter of personal responsibility and ideology, as in the case of Bill Gates and George Soros, poverty alleviation has many proponents who don't necessarily agree on the best strategy for the future.

RECONCILING THE DIFFERENT
APPROACHES TO POVERTY ALLEVIATION

The most obvious and widely publicized ideological and strategic clash has been between the intergovernmental organizations (IGOs) and the loosely aligned medley of anti-globalization groups who argue that the IGOs' policies are hurting the poor more than helping them.

Outside the headline-grabbing issues that caused such widely publicized protests in Seattle in 1999, Washington D.C. in 2000 and 2002, Genoa in 2001, and other cities where the World Trade Organization (WTO), International Monetary Fund (IMF), or G8 nations met, the issues can be summed up as different views on poverty and different strategies for eradicating it (Figure 7.1).

Perceptions of Poverty

For a long time, IGOs and national governments have defined poverty as the lack of some kind of resources, be it money, food, shelter, heath services, or other. To this day, the World Bank, the IMF, and other IGOs measure poverty in terms of the strict $1 a day or $2 a day thresholds delineating absolute and relative poverty. Furthermore, some observers[224] argue that governments and governmental organizations (in this case, the U.K. government and the EU) often view poverty only as a result of the internal political and social workings of developing countries, and not as a part of the larger, global forces reshaping the economic landscape. Therefore, their solutions to poverty inevitably prescribe market liberalization reforms, democratic reforms, and other changes geared towards fuller integration of the developing countries into the global economy. Economic development is seen as the most effective and efficient cure for poverty, regardless of the country's history or current social, economic, or political conditions.

Figure 7.1 The protests at the World Trade Organization meeting in Seattle in 1999 drew world attention through the large numbers of protestors and the intensity of their activities. The women shown here dangled for about an hour, holding up a banner at the side of the Interstate 5 freeway to protest the upcoming meeting.

On the other hand, many **non-governmental organizations (NGOs)** regard poverty as a multidimensional and relative phenomenon, influenced by a number of factors, including gender, ethnicity, education level, location, and citizenship.[225]

More importantly, many NGOs have proposed that poverty is a direct result of globalization and the ill-conceived reforms forced on developing countries by IGOs and the rich nations that control them. One author even dubs the phenomenon "globalized poverty," and argues that to conquer it, new rules are needed for the functioning of states, markets, and social and regional networks, and the management of the economy and the environment.[226] In general, many NGOs and anti-globalization groups advocate that to combat poverty on a global scale, a much broader set of reforms would be needed—reforms that not only spur development and progress in the developing countries, but also give them leverage and defense against the lopsided, protectionist policies of the developed nations.

Causes of the Clash

The collision between these diverse points of views is expressed in many different ways—from disruptive and sometimes violent street demonstrations, to fiery editorials in newspapers, websites, and other media, to polemics on college campuses and scholarly journals.

One of the overarching points of contention between the supranational organizations and the anti-globalization move-ment is the perceived imbalance of power within the international institutions such as the WTO, the UN, the World Bank, and the IMF. The groups opposing these institutions claim that they are nothing more than tools in the hands of a few powerful and rich Western nations and corporations who use them to exploit the poorer countries' labor and resources for their own benefit. The academic Ikubolajeh Logan goes as far as to compare globaliza-tion to colonialism, claiming that hiding behind such lofty causes as the promotion of democracy and human rights, the "global forces use their unrivaled supremacy both to perpetuate their political and economic domination and to undermine Third World empowerment."[227]

The most frequent examples given in defense of this claim are the structural adjustment programs (SAPs) recommended by the IGOs and the undemocratic and biased structures and voting rights at the WTO and the UN, for example. The SAPs, which were originally designed as a way for indebted nations to repay their debts to the international community, in practice often result in the cutting of funds for national programs for poverty reduction, health care, and child education and sparked many civil protests throughout the developing world. The WTO, a 148-nation member organization and the UN, a world organization with representatives from 191 national governments, do have tiered voting rights that give more power to the larger and more economically strong nations.

Other issues on which the IGOs and the NGOs often have similar goals but disagree on the strategies to reach them include environmental preservation, gender rights, debt relief, AIDS eradication, trade policy reform, and many other diverse global causes. While these disagreements are ultimately seen as healthy, the international institutions argue that their opposition's tactics often backfire on the same poor people they are trying to help. Sebastian Mallaby describes how the World Bank has had to abandon its support for dozens of poverty alleviation projects in developing countries because of opposition from various Western activist groups who claimed that the projects would harm the environment, displace people, or cause other damages. The author claims that because of their actions, the projects are cancelled despite the locals' need for them, or they proceed without the Bank's watchful eye ensuring that its high environmental and anti-corruption standards, for example, are followed. Ultimately, Mallaby argues,

> However noble many of the activists' motives, and however flawed the big institutions' record, this constant campaigning threatens to disable not just the World Bank but regional development banks and governmental aid organizations such as

the U.S. Agency for International Development. If this takes place, the world may lose the potential for good that big organizations offer: to rise above the single-issue advocacy that small groups tend to pursue and to square off against humanity's grandest problems." [228]

Reconciliation and Amendment

Regardless of how others view them, the NGOs have found their role as an informal system of checks and balances against powerful international organizations. In fact, many globalization proponents and the IGOs themselves have acknowledged the value in some of the activists' opinions and the need for reforms within the global institutions.

One of the biggest proponents of constructive dialogue between the parties has been none other than the outgoing president of the World Bank, James Wolfensohn. He has consistently asked for the activist groups' input, arranged meetings with their leaders, and charged internal commissions with advocating the opposition's view on World Bank policies.[229]

Although many anti-globalization groups remain fiercely reticent, others, such as Oxfam, World Vision, and the World Wildlife Fund, have agreed to cooperate with IGOs. Consequently, they have been able to push for the incorporation of many more clear and stringent standards for the World Bank's operations in developing countries and have succeeded in implementing many of them. However, the uncompromising positions taken by the NGOs in regard to the intergovernmental organizations, as well as their anti-globalization positions, have made their relationship with the World Bank tenuous and costly for the World Bank at times.[230]

No one can deny the overall positive influence these groups have had on the policies and actions of the IGOs. A certain gradual softening of the conditions and growing consideration for local input and circumstances has marked the strategies of the IMF and the World Bank in recent years. This desire for reconciliation has opened the door to a range of new

approaches to poverty alleviation within the international institutions and beyond.

NEW APPROACHES TO POVERTY ALLEVIATION

Besides pressure from NGOs, other factors contributing to the
evolving nature of the fight on poverty include continuous
research on poverty at various institutions; changing political
and economic conditions, especially the trend towards new
regional alliances; the emergence of new threats (such as
terrorism); and the emergence of new allies (such as wealthy
donors like Bill Gates, Ted Turner, and George Soros).
Collectively, these factors are just beginning to have an impact
on the war on poverty. It is likely that their influence will only
increase with time.

New Approaches at the IGOs

The most significant development in the IGOs' strategy for
poverty alleviation has been the adoption in 1999 of a new
Comprehensive Development Framework (CDF). This framework calls for four major adjustments in the operational mode
of the institutions: (1) to adopt a more "holistic," long-term
approach to poverty reduction, (2) to put the affected countries
in control of their own poverty alleviation strategies, (3) to partner with governments and other global and local forces with the
same agenda, and (4) to emphasize tangible results as the only
measure of success for each project.[231]

The international community points to the CDF as the best
approach to poverty alleviation because it takes into consideration the multidimensional nature of poverty and attempts to fix
it accordingly by attacking the problems on all "social, structural,
human, governance, environmental, economic, and financial
levels simultaneously." [232]

The main instruments for achieving the goals of the CDF
have become the Poverty Reduction Strategy Papers (PRSPs).
These papers, written by each individual country, are designed

to spell out its government's strategy for combating poverty in terms of the planned processes and steps, the diagnostics used to determine them, the costs associated with implementing them, and the proper indicators that will be used for monitoring their progress.[233] Today, PRSPs are a requirement for receiving just about any kind of assistance from the World Bank and the IMF, including debt relief. Over 70 developing countries have used them or plan to use them in the near future.[234]

Another goal of the CDF is to better align the often disparate partners in the war on poverty, such as governments, donors, civil society, the private sector, and other development stakeholders.[235] Designed to increase the efficiency and effectiveness of international support, this goal shows, once again, the movement within the IGOs towards greater accountability, responsiveness, and cooperation with outside groups.

This new trend within IGOs has been noted by some observers for its similarity to the management practices of business corporations, and that observation rings even more true when considering the final emphasis of the CDF on specific and measurable results.

Gaby Ramia, for example, examines the link between global social policy and strategic management in international organizations and finds that "global social policy analysts can benefit from the systematic assessment of management changes such as the increasing use of cross-sectoral alliances (between the public, non-profit, and for-profit sectors), the growing importance of contractual tools, and the heightened sense in which organizational redesign shapes social objectives."[236]

Clearly, IGOs have come a long way since the "shock therapy" approach of instant price liberalization, spending cutbacks and currency devaluation that they recommended as a way to global market integration for Latin American countries in the 1980s and for Central and Eastern European countries in the early 1990s. Only time will tell whether the new CDF approach will prove to be more effective and less painful for developing nations.

New Approaches in Developed Countries

A new era has begun in foreign aid disbursement and management by governments. Gone are the times when developed
countries would give loans and grants to developing countries
without asking many questions or following up to see the results
of their assistance. Accountability—on both sides—is the new
motto, and it comes not a moment too soon. As a *Business Week*
article pointed out, "far too much of the $10 billion the United
States calls 'foreign aid' goes to nations such as Egypt and
Pakistan for political reasons rather than to seriously promote
economic development."[237] To be effective in the fight against
poverty, countries have to learn to better manage their aid
dollars, continues the article. The different agencies have to
stop duplicating their work, stop simply writing off bad debt,
begin demanding more responsibility and better planning on
the side of the recipients, and begin following up on their side
to ensure that the money is spent where it should be.

Increasing the value and rationality of U.S. assistance has
become a priority for the U.S. Agency for International
Development (USAID) (Figure 7.2). In a 2004 position paper,
it points to its new focus on clearer goals, better allocation,
emphasis on building strong local institutions, closer partner-
ships with the host countries, improved coordination with
other donors, and several other priorities designed to improve
its effectiveness.[238]

For its part, the EU is also looking to streamline its own
assistance programs and those of its member states. In its 2004
report, EuropeAid asserts that its reform initiative, started in 2000,
is progressing on the objectives of moving management of the
poverty alleviation programs to the EU field offices in the respec-
tive countries, eliminating some of the bureaucracy prevalent in
its operations, and shifting to more results-oriented actions.[239]

Furthermore, European foreign ministers are discussing
changes to the long-time practice of tying foreign aid to purchase of goods and services from the donor country, a practice

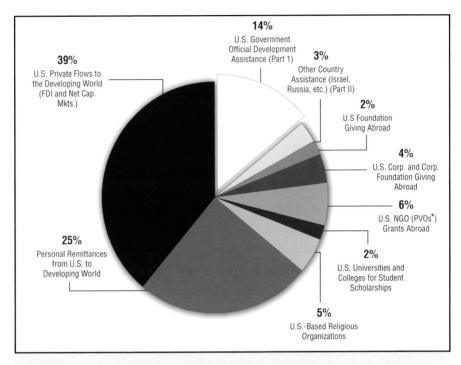

Figure 7.2 U.S. Resource Flows to the developing world, which in 2000 were nearly $70.5 billion, have been gradually shifting from predominantly government aid to resources from private and public-private alliances, which now account for the majority of the total flows. This new model allows for more responsibility, efficiency, and accountability by all aid stakeholders.

* Private Voluntary Organizations

Source: U.S. Agency for International Development

that has been discredited as catering to big-business interests and diminishing the effectiveness of the aid by at least 25 percent.[240] Other proposals being considered include moving from a more reactive to more proactive approach to trade expansion with developing countries and faster response to the changing environment of international trade.[241]

New Approaches at Multinational Corporations

Wary of repeating their mistakes from the last decade, when many companies such as Nike, Reebok, Gap, and others were criticized for using child labor, paying poverty-rate wages, and maintaining sweatshop conditions in their Third World factories, multinational corporations (MNCs) now are changing the way they do business.

Long scornful of rules and regulations imposed on them by governments and other organizations, businesses are opening up to self-regulation and public accountability on their human rights records. In the last few years, more and more MNCs have officially assumed corporate responsibility and self-monitoring functions designed to prevent human rights abuses and promote worker's rights and ethical standards in their own or their suppliers' production facilities.

Many have begun to issue social responsibility reports that show the company's support for ethical standards, fair wages, and organized labor, among other things, and to showcase its support for social causes such as poverty alleviation, community development, and similar initiatives. Since 2000, nearly 1,780 global companies have joined the UN Global Compact, a newly formed network of businesses, NGOs, labor unions, and other institutions that seek to promote good corporate citizenship.[242]

Other forms of self-regulation and prevention of human rights abuses is the increasingly popular practice of using labels to mark products made in decent working conditions. One of the oldest such labeling programs is RUGMARK, which started originally in India as a monitoring and certifying operation against child labor abuses. The RUGMARK label assures the buyer that children were not employed in the making of the rug. The organization has expanded its scope to many other production countries, such as Nepal and Pakistan, and consumer countries such as Germany, United States, Canada, and others. Today, over 260 rug makers in India alone have signed for the program, and hundreds of other exporters and merchants use it.[243] Similar labeling programs are used to ensure the fair treatment for farmers and factory workers in Third World countries. Partnering with the NGOs that run them, such as the FairTrade,

TRANSFAIR, Abrinq, and others, is becoming more and more popular among progressive companies like Starbucks, Reebok, and Nordstrom that realize that fighting poverty by using fair trade standards is not only good for the company's reputation, but also for its bottom line.

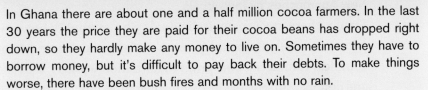

Kuapa Kokoo Producers' Co-operative, Ghana

In Ghana there are about one and a half million cocoa farmers. In the last 30 years the price they are paid for their cocoa beans has dropped right down, so they hardly make any money to live on. Sometimes they have to borrow money, but it's difficult to pay back their debts. To make things worse, there have been bush fires and months with no rain.

About ten years ago one group of cocoa farmers joined together to form a group called Kuapa Kokoo. This means 'The Good Coca Farmers Company.' They sell some of their cocoa through Fairtrade. This means they get more money for each sack of beans.

The Kuapa Kokoo farmers can use the extra income from Fairtrade for training and to buy farming tools to help with their work. They learn how to look after their environment and grow their cocoa without using harmful chemicals.

Kuapa Kokoo includes both women and men farmers—there are now far more women working in the organization and making important decisions.

Kuapa Kokoo trains its farmers so they know how to weigh and bag their beans. This had been a problem because some cocoa buyers would cheat the farmers by using inaccurate scales that didn't weigh fairly.

Kuapa Kokoo farmers are able to learn about the foods that are best for them to eat, about health and childcare. They have new water pumps for clean water too.

The farmers also learn about managing their money and how to make extra money in the 'hungry season' when the cocoa is growing—for example by making soap from the cocoa husks, which means a waste product is being recycled!

More and more villages want to join Kuapa Kokoo, but at the moment they can't sell all their cocoa beans through Fairtrade—there still isn't enough demand for Fairtrade chocolate in the UK."

Source: FairTrade, *http://www.fairtrade.org.uk/downloads/pdf/fairtradeinyourschool.pdf*, p.13.

The driver behind this business movement has been the need for self-preservation as much as the desire to help developing countries. By taking these preemptive actions, business may spare themselves another round of government-imposed regulations or negative public campaigns launched by anti-globalization NGOs. Nevertheless, the final result of this strategy is more fair trade, better working conditions, and better pay for the millions of poor workers in developing countries.

New Approaches by Individuals

Finally, there are a many individuals who exemplify how one person can truly make a difference in the world. These are the countless volunteers, non-profit organization workers, activists, and donors who selflessly are giving their time, money, and efforts to help alleviate poverty in some of the most desperate and dangerous countries around the world. While volunteerism and philanthropy are not new, the approach taken by some of the new crop of **philanthropists** is rather extraordinary.

Microsoft chairman Bill Gates and financier George Soros are examples of what *Business Week* calls "a new breed of philanthropist . . . spearheading the most recent assaults on poverty."[244] These are individuals who undertake poverty alleviation projects with the same zest, discipline, and savvy as they do their business deals (Table 7.1). Their focus, practical approach, and, not the least, exceptional generosity have brought hope and help for millions of poor people around the world who can't afford proper health care and education (the focus of the Bill and Melinda Gates Foundation) or who need assistance with building economic development, good governance, and human rights protection (the focus of the Soros Foundation Network).

Philip and Donna Berber, have given $100 million from the proceeds of the sale of their high-tech company to fund A Glimmer of Hope, a foundation helping the poor of Ethiopia.[245] Oprah Winfrey's foundation is spending over $20 million to

Table 7.1 The 10 Most Generous Philanthropists

RANK	NAME	BACKGROUND	2000–2004 GIVEN OR PLEDGED (MILLIONS)	CAUSES	ESTIMATED LIFETIME GIVING (MILLIONS)	REMAINING NET WORTH (MILLIONS)	GIVING AS A % OF NET WORTH
1	Bill and Melinda Gates	Microsoft co-founder	$10,085	Health, education, info. access	27,976	48,000	58%
2	Gordon and Betty Moore	Intel co-founder	7,046	Environmental conservation, science	7,300	3,800	192
3	Warren Buffett	Berkshire Hathaway CEO	2,721	Reproductive choice, reducing nukes	2,730	41,000	8
4	George Soros	Investor	2,301	Open and free societies	5,171	7,200	72
5	James and Virginia Stowers	American Century founder	1,346	Biomedical research	1,564	716	218
6	Eli and Edythe Broad	SunAmerica, KB Home founder	1,333	Public education, arts, science	1,570	6,000	26
7	Michael and Susan Dell	Dell founder	933	Children's health and education	1,230	14,200	9
8	Alfred Mann	Medical devices	830	Biomedical education and research	1,000	1,400	71
9	Paul Allen	Microsoft co-founder	735	Arts, culture	831	20,000	4
10	Walton Family	Family of Wal-Mart founder	650	Education	1,000	95,800	1

build a Leadership Academy for Girls in South Africa.[246] Ted Turner has pledged $1 billion to the United Nations to promote "a more peaceful, prosperous, and just world."[247]

The war against global poverty needs the support of all these organizations, institutions, and people now more than ever. Only with such newly invigorated efforts can the world accomplish at least some of the lofty objectives set in the Millennium

Development Goals. And while the MDGs are not an end in and of themselves, they are, in a nutshell, a representation of humanity's condition at the beginning of the 21st century, with all its ideals, struggles, and hopes for the future. The fact that poverty reduction is the first goal underlines its crucial importance for the future of our civilization. Will the forces of globalization help us tackle poverty or will they exacerbate it? As with any major shift in our history, it is likely that the final outcome will surprise us.

Corruption—An activity through which a public official abuses his or her power for personal benefit. Examples of corrupt activities include bribery, extortion, embezzlement, and nepotism.

Coup d'etat—The sudden and often violent overthrow of a government by a small group of people, usually military or government personnel.

Economic growth—An increase in the production of goods and services in a country, usually due to innovation, technological advances, trade, increase in productivity, or similar factors.

Exchange rate controls—Government restrictions placed on a currency with the purpose of maintaining its value relatively stable and preventing currency speculation.

Fiscal reforms—Changes in the government's rules and regulations related to taxes and government spending.

Free trade areas—Specially designated areas in a country (usually around ports or other major transportation hubs) where business can be conducted without or with less restrictions such as taxes, import/export duties, and tariffs.

Gross domestic product (GDP)—The value of all goods and services produced within the boundaries of a country. GDP calculations do not include imported goods, but they do include the goods produced within a country by foreign companies or investors.

Green revolution—A wave of scientific discoveries in genetics, biology, chemistry, and technology that resulted in a dramatic increase in crop productivity, especially in East and Southeast Asia and Latin America.

Income supplements—Benefits usually given by governments to supplement the income of poor people in order to bring it up to a certain minimum level established by law. Supplements can be monetary or in the form of food stamps, for example.

Inflation—The gradual (or, in more unstable economies, sudden) increase in the price of goods and services, which results in the decrease of the national currency's value. In the United States, inflation is usually monitored through the Consumer Price Index or the Producer Price Index.

Informal Economy—A system of exchange of goods and/or services that functions outside the state-controlled economic activity. Examples include barter, street-trading, odd jobs, etc.

Intergovernmental organizations (IGOs)—Institutions formed by the formal agreement of three or more countries that have a formal structure and perform ongoing activities. The most well-known IGOs include the United Nations, the World Trade Organization (WTO), and the International Monetary Fund (IMF). Also called supranational organizations.

Loan subsidies—Financial assistance usually provided by governments to other governments, individuals, or organizations.

Non-governmental organizations (NGOs)—Theoretically, any organization that exists outside the government and relies on some form of private funding for operation. In the context of this book, NGOs are referred to primarily as the non-profit, non-commercial organizations whose political and/or social goals and principles revolve around opposition to the globalization process.

Philanthropist—A person who donates funds, property, or personal efforts to improve the well-being of others.

Purchasing power parity (PPP)—A method used to calculate the equivalent of a specific amount of money in different currencies. PPP is often used to compare standards of living across different countries.

Market economy—An economic system that functions solely based on the laws of supply and demand, without much government regulation.

Per capita income—The average income for one person in a country's population. Per capita income is often used to measure the standard of living in a country.

Poverty Reduction Strategy Papers (PRSPs)—Documents that describe the macroeconomic, structural and social policies and programs as well as the external financing that a country will pursue over several years to promote broad-based growth and reduce poverty.

Recession—A period during which the economic activity of a country or region declines. Recession usually is expressed in terms of a decrease in GDP.

Short-term investors—Generally, investors who are looking for quick profit and are ready to change their investment holding as soon as it makes some profit or if they see the slightest sign of possible decline in value. Short-term investors usually like to speculate and change their investment portfolio frequently, increasing the volatility of markets.

Sovereignty—The independence of a country (or its government) to make its own decisions and act of its own will, without outside interference.

Standard of living—A popular measure of the financial well-being of the people of a country, as expressed in their ability to purchase goods and services.

Structural adjustment programs (SAPs)—Projects undertaken by national governments in partnership with the World Bank or International Monetary Fund, to reallocate resources and change the structure of production and employment of a national economy to reflect changing economic policies or trading conditions.

Supranational organizations—Voluntary organizations whose members are usually different countries (represented by their governments). Also called intergovernmental organizations (IGOs). Examples of such entities include the United Nations, the World Trade Organization (WTO), and others.

Trade barriers—Restrictions on international trade activities, usually placed by governments. Most common trade barriers are custom duties, import/export taxes, and tariffs. Other non-financial trade barriers are different technology standards, for example, or import or export quotas on certain products, both of which restrict the flow of imported goods or services.

Trade liberalization—The general relaxation of trade regulations and requirements with the purpose to stimulate more international trade.

Trade quotas—Limits on the quantity of certain products that can be imported or exported in a certain period to or from a country.

Welfare state—A social system, or the country in which such system exists, where the government assumes responsibility for the welfare of its citizens, especially in the areas of health care, education, employment, and social security.

1 Anonymous, "Bakyt: Missing Out on School and Play Because of Poverty," case study, copyright Childhood Poverty Research and Policy Centre. Available online at http://www.childhoodpoverty .org/index.php?action=casestudy&id= 137. Reprinted with permission.

2 United Nations, "United Nations Millennium Declaration," 8 September 2000. Available online at http://www .un.org/millennium/declaration/ares55 2e.htm.

3 United Nations, *United Nations Millennium Assembly Website.* Available online at http://www.un.org/millennium.

4 The World Bank Group, *Millennium Development Goals: Malnutrition and Hunger.* Available online at http://www.developmentgoals.org/Pov erty.htm.

5 United Nations Development Programme Evaluation Office, *Monitoring Poverty.* Essentials: Synthesis of Lessons Learned, # 10, May 2003.Available online at http://www.undp.org/eo/ documents/essentials/Monitoring Poverty.pdf.

6 U.S. Census Bureau, Highlights, *Global Population Profile: 2002,* 3. Available online at http://www.census.gov/ ipc/prod/wp02/wp-02001.pdf.

7 Glossary, *Commanding Heights: The Battle for the World Economy."* Available online at http://www.pbs .org/wgbh/commandingheights/shared /glossary/g.html.

8 "Eradication of Poverty: Basis for Action and Objectives," *The Copenhagen Declaration and Programme of Action.* World Summit for Social Development, United Nations, 1995. Available online at http://www.visionoffice.com/socdev/ wssdpa-2.htm.

9 United Nations Development Programme, *Human Development Reports: Do You Know That,* Goal 1: Poverty and Hunger. Available online at http://hdr.undp.org/reports/ global/2003/know_that.html#2.

10 United Nations Development Programme, Overview, *Human Development Report 2003,* 2. Available online at http://hdr.undp.org/reports/ global/2003/pdf/2003/hdr03_overview .pdf.

11 Moisés Naím, "An Indigenous World," *Foreign Policy,* 1 November 2003. Available online at http://www .foreignpolicy.com/story/files/ story181.php.

12 Daniel Yergin, "Threats to Globalisation in an Unstable World," *London Sunday Telegraph,* 9 March 2003. Available online at http://www .telegraph.co.uk/money/main.jhtml?x ml=%2Fmoney%2F2003%2F03%2F09 %2Fccglobl09.xml.

13 Pete Engardio et al., "Special Report: Global Poverty," *Business Week,* 14 October 2002, 114–118.

14 United Nations Development Programme. *Human Development Reports: Do You Know That.*

15 Joseph Stiglitz, *Globalization and Its Discontents.* New York: W. W. Norton & Company, 2002, pp. 6–7.

16 Anup Shah, "Structural Adjustments— A Major Cause of Poverty," *Global Issues.org,* 16 July 2003. Available online at http://www.globalissues.org/ TradeRelated/SAP.asp#EarnMore EatLess.

17 Thomas C. Dawson, "Stiglitz, the IMF, and Globalization," *Transition* (May-June 2002), 12–13.

18 Philippe Rekacewicz, "Main Causes of Poverty in the World" chart, published in *Global Environment Outlook 2000.* London: Unep-Earthscan, 1999, p. 15.Available online at http://www.povertymap.net/ mapsgraphics/index.cfm?data _id=12973&theme=poverty%20 indicators.

19 OECD, "Poverty-Environment-Gender Linkages", pre-print of the *DAC Journal* 2:4 (2001): IV–21. Available online at http://www.oecd.org/dataoecd/47/46/1960506.pdf.

20 Development Assistance Committee, "Executive Summary." *In the Face of Poverty: Meeting the Global Challenge through Partnership*, DAC Guidelines on Poverty Reduction, OECD (2001): 9. Available online at http://www.oecd.org/dataoecd/18/19/1849018.pdf.

21 Caterina Ruggeri Laderchi et al. *"Does it matter that we don't agree on the definition of poverty?: A comparison of four approaches."* Oxford: International Development Center, 2003. Available online at http://www2.qeh.ox.ac.uk/pdf/qehwp/qehwps107.pdf.

22 International Development Research Center, "Take a Closer Look at Poverty," 10 January 2003. Available online at http://network.idrc.ca/ev.php?URL_ID=26048&URL_DO=DO_TOPIC&URL_SECTION=201&reload=1058151529.

23 *Global Poverty Report 2001: A Globalized Market Opportunities and Risks for the Poor*, G8 Summit, Genoa, July 2001, p. 4. Available online at http://www.adb.org/Documents/Reports/Global_Poverty/2001/GPR2001.pdf.

24 Environment News Service, "World Bank Concerns Overshadowed by Terrorism, Iraq," 26 April 2004. Available online at http://www.keepmedia.com/pubs/EnvironmentNewsService/2004/04/26/455304.

25 OECD, "DAC Guidelines on Poverty Reduction," Executive summary excerpt. Available online at http://www.oecd.org/document/1/0,2340,en_2649_34621_1885953_1_1_1_37445,00.html.

26 James D. Wolfesohn. "Closing Remarks" at Scaling Up Poverty Reduction: A Global Learning Process and Conference, Shanghai, (27 May, 2004). Available online at http://www.worldbank.org/wbi/reducingpoverty/docs/confDocs/JDWShanghaiClosing.pdf.

27 Paul E. Lovejoy *Transformations in Slavery*, Cambridge: Cambridge University Press, 2000, derived from Tables 4.1, 3.4, and 7.4. Quoted in "Transatlantic Slave Trade: Origins of Slaves," About online database. Available online at http://africanhistory.about.com/library/bl/bl-slavery-stats4.htm#table.

28 Jeffrey D. Sachs et al., "Ending Africa's Poverty Trap / Comments and Discussion," *Brookings Papers on Economic Activity* 1 (2004): 117.

29 Matt Rosenberg, "The Colonization of the Continent by European Powers," Berlin Conference of 1884–1885 to Divide Africa. Available online at http://geography.about.com/cs/politicalgeog/a/berlinconferenc.htm.

30 Sachs, "Ending Africa's Poverty Trap," 117.

31 Ikaweba Bunting, "The Heart of Africa," *New Internationalist*, Special supplement, January 1999. Available online at http://www.newint.org/issue309/anticol.htm.

32 Sachs, "Ending Africa's Poverty Trap," 117.

33 George Saitoti, "Reflections on African Development," *Journal of Third World Studies* 20, 2 (Fall 2003): 13.

34 ThinkQuest team 16645, *The Living Africa: About Our Site-Overview*, online, Thinkquest Library 1998. Available online at http://library.thinkquest.org/16645/overview.shtml.

35 Miguel Edward and Mary Kay Gugerty, *Ethnic Diversity, Social Sanctions, and Public Goods in Kenya*, Available online at http://emlab.berkeley.edu/users/emiguel/miguel_tribes.pdf.

36 United Nations Development Programme, "Overview: Cultural Liberty in Today's Diverse World," *Human Development Report 2004.* Available online at http://hdr.undp .org/reports/global/2004/pdf/hdr04 _overview.pdf.

37 Mike Wooldridge, "UN Warns of Ethnic Diversity Timebomb," *BBC News,* 15 July 2004, UK edition. Available online at http://news.bbc.co .uk/1/hi/world/africa/3897479.stm.

38 Saitoti, "Reflections on African Development, " 13.

39 Sachs, "Ending Africa's Poverty Trap," 117.

40 The World Bank Group, *Global Economic Prospects 2004—Realizing the Development Promise of the Doha Agenda,* 2004 ed., "Appendix 1 - Regional Economic Prospects," 249. Available online at http://www .worldbank.org/prospects/gep2004/ appendix1.pdf.

41 Saitoti, "Reflections on African Development," 13.

42 Jeffrey D. Sachs, "A Rich Nation, A Poor Continent," The *New York Times,* 9 July 2003, A21.

43 UNAIDS, Regional Analysis, *Sub-Saharan Africa.* Available online at http://www.unaids.org/Unaids/EN/ Geographical+area/By+Region/ Sub-Saharan+Africa.asp#.

44 UN, "AIDS Orphans in Sub-Saharan Africa: A Looming Threat to Future Generations," *10 Stories the World Should Hear More About.* Available online at http://www.un.org/events/ tenstories/story.asp?storyID=400.

45 UN, "Excerpts from the Report: Combating HIV/AIDS, Malaria and Tuberculosis," *Economic Report on Africa 2003.* Available online at http://www.un.org/ecosocdev/geninfo/ afrec/newrels/eraexcp.htm.

46 Sachs, "Ending Africa's Poverty Trap," 117.

47 United Nations Population Fund, "Population and Poverty," *State of World Population 2004.* Available online at http://www.unfpa.org/swp/ 2004/english/ch2/index.htm.

48 United Nations Population Fund, "Selected Demographic Trends," *Sub-Saharan Africa: Demographic Indicators,* 2004. Available online at http://www.unfpa.org/africa/ demographic.htm.

49 Ibid.

50 Norwegian Refugee Council, "Internal Displacement in Africa," *Global IDP Project,* January 2004. Available online at http://www.idpproject.org/regions/ Africa_idps.htm.

51 Roberta Cohen, "Internal Displacement in Africa: Where Does the Responsibility Lie?" *Global Politics,* 26 May 2004. Available online at http://www.brookings.edu/fp/projects/ idp/20040526rcohen.htm.

52 Daniel Cohen, *The Wealth of the World and the Poverty of Nations,* trans. Jacqueline Lindenfeld. Cambridge and London: The MIT Press, 1998), p. 6.

53 The World Bank Group, *Global Economic Prospects,* 250.

54 Ian Gary and Terry Lynn Karl, "Executive Summary," *Bottom of the Barrel: Africa's Oil Boom and the Poor,* Catholic Relief Services, June 2003. Available online at http://www .catholicrelief.org/get_involved/ advocacy/policy_and_strategic_issues/ oil_report.cfm.

55 N. Roberto Zagha and Oleksiy Shvets, "*Shanghai Conference: Scaling Up Poverty Reduction: Lessons and Challenges from China, Indonesia, Korea and Malaysia,*" The World Bank Group. Available online at http://lnweb18.worldbank.org/eap/ eap.nsf/Attachments/Special+Focus+ April+2004/$File/Focus+final+April04 .pdf.

56 Zagha and Shvets, 3.

57 Mari Pangestu, "*The Social Impact of Globalisation in Southeast Asia*," Working paper #187, OECD Development Centre, December 2001. Available online at http://www.oecd.org/dataoecd/9/59/27 31385.pdf.

58 Amy Chua, *World on Fire: How Exporting Free Market Democracy Breeds Ethnic Hatred and Global Instability.* New York: Doubleday, 2003, pp. 136, 151.

59 Asia Development Bank, "Poverty Remains a Major Challenge Despite Asia's High Growth" (press release, 26 Aug. 2004.) Available online at http://adb.org/Documents/News/2004/nr2004093.asp.

60 Asian Development Bank, "4.1 Recent Estimates and Trends in Poverty," *Key Indicators 2004: Poverty in Asia: Measurements, Estimates and Prospects* report. Available online at http://adb.org/Documents/Books/Key_ Indicators/2004/pdf/Special-Chapter -2004.pdf.

61 Mike Wallace, "The Plight of North Korea," *60 Minutes* transcript, 20 July 2003. Available online at http://www.cbsnews.com/stories/2003/ 07/16/60minutes/main563623.shtml? CMP=ILC-SearchStories.

62 Associated Press, "North Korea Needs More Food, UN Says," *The Globe and Mail.com*, 21 October 2004. Available online at http://www.theglobeandmail .com/servlet/story/RTGAM.20041021. wnkor1021/BNStory/International.

63 Ibid, 39.

64 Thomas Friedman, Interview with Ray Suarez, 12 August 2002, NewsHour with Jim Lehrer transcript. Available online at http://www.pbs.org/newshour/ bb/foreign_correspondence/july- dec02/tom_8-12.html.

65 "Benefits of High Growth Must Reach Poor in South Asia, Says ADB Vice- President," Asian Development Bank.

Press Release, 16 Sep. 2004. Available online at http://adb.org/Documents/ News/INRM/inrm200402.asp.

66 Asian Development Bank, 31.

67 Mostafizur Rahman, "South Asia in the Current Context," *OECD Policies Towards Development of Developing Countries: Learning from East Asia, Lessons for South Asia*, OECD Seminar. Available online at http://www.oecd .org/dataoecd/36/58/31799439.pdf.

68 Ibid.

69 Sharier Khan, "Poverty, Unemployment Stunts South Asia's Growth Graph,"OneWorld.com article, 1 April 2004. Available online at http://southasia.oneworld.net/article/ view/82908/1/?PrintableVersion= enabled.

70 Asian Human Rights Commission, *Exploitation: Child Illiteracy and Child Labour Are the Continent's Main Social Ills*, Report. 29 September 2004. Available online at http://acr.hrschool .org/mainfile.php/0197/367/?Print=yes.

71 Richard Pomfret, *Central Asia Since 1991: The Experience of the New Independent States*, OECD Development Centre Working Paper No: 212 (July 2003).Available online at http://www.oecd.org/dataoecd/23/58/ 5961227.pdf.

72 Ibid.

73 Caroline Lambert, "At the Crossroads," *The Economist*, 24 July 2003. Available online at http://www.economist.com/ surveys/PrinterFriendly.cfm?Story_ID =1922562.

74 IRIN News, "Central Asia: High Child Poverty despite Economic Growth–UNICEF," Reuters Foundation AlertNet website, 14 Oct 2004. Available online at http://www.alertnet .org/thenews/newsdesk/IRIN/0c8db43 37cc27a7900c6284f88ba0fe7.htm.

75 The World Bank, *The Millennium Development Goals in Europe and*

Central Asia, 2003. Available online at http://siteresources.worldbank.org/IN TECA/Publications/20219571/MDGs. pdf.

76 Asian Development Bank, 31.

77 ADB, *Working Together to Fight Poverty*, November 2003. Available online at http://adb.org/Documents/ Events/2003/CAREC/Second_Ministeri al_Conference/central_asia.pdf.

78 UNDP, "The Region Is Richer than It Is Developed," *Arab Human Development Report 2002*, press kit. Available online at http://www.undp.org/rbas/ahdr/ ahdr1/presskit1/PR1.pdf.

79 Ibid, 1.

80 "Executive Summary," *UNDP Releases the First Arab Human Development Report*, press kit. Available online at http://www.undp.org/rbas/ahdr/ahdr1/ presskit1/PRExecSummary.pdf.

81 "The Poor Arab Street," Global Agenda, Economist.com, 3 July 2002. Available online at http://www.economist .com/agenda/displaystory.cfm?story_ id=1212573.

82 UNDP, "The Region is Richer than It Is Developed," 2.

83 UNDP, "Goal 1: Eradicate Extreme Poverty and Hunger," *The Millennium Development Goals in Arab Countries: Towards 2015: Achievements and Aspirations*, 2003. Available online at http://www.undp.org/mdg/Arab_ RegionalReport_english.pdf.

84 Info–Prod Strategic Business Information, "Poverty Lower Than 9%," *Info-Prod Research (Middle East)* wire feed. Ramat-Gan: Oct 13, 2004. Available online at http://www.infoprod.co.il

85 Robert Looney, "Book Review of *Earnings Inequality, Unemployment and Poverty in the Middle East and North America*," *Journal of Third World Studies* 19.2 (2002): 319.

86 United Nations, "Extreme Poverty," *Millennium Development Goals: Report for the Kingdom of Saudi Arabia 2002*. Available online at http://www.undp .org/mdg/saudi.pdf.

87 UNDP, "Goal 1: Eradicate Extreme Poverty and Hunger," 5.

88 Xinhua Agency, "Chinese President Confident in Asia's Future," *China Through a Lens*, 24 April 2004. Available online at http://www.china .org.cn/english/2004/Apr/93899.htm.

89 World Bank, "Europe and Central Asia: An Overview," *The Millennium Development Goals in Europe and Central Asia*, 2003. Available online at http://siteresources.worldbank.org/INT ECA/Publications/20219571/MDGs.pdf.

90 World Bank, *Making Transition Work for Everyone: Poverty and Inequality in Europe and Central Asia*. Quoted in "Strategy, Implementation and Outcome," *Economies in Transition: an OED Evaluation of World Bank Assistance*, May 2004. Available online at http://siteresources.worldbank.org/ INTECA/Resources/transition_ economies.pdf.

91 IFAD, "Executive Summary: Regional Overview", *Assessment of Rural Poverty: Central and Eastern Europe and the Newly Independent States*, 2002. Available online at http://www.ifad .org/poverty/region/pn/PN_e_1.pdf.

92 Ibid.

93 Ibid.

94 European Commission/The World Bank, "What Is the Economic Situation in the Region?" *Economic Reconstruction and Development in South East Europe*. Available online at http://www.seerecon.org/gen/econsitut ation.htm.

95 Antonis Adam, Theodora S. Kosma, and Jimmy McHugh, "Introduction," *Trade-Liberalization Strategies: What Could Southeastern Europe Learn from the CEFTA and BFTA?* IMF working

paper, Dec. 2003. Available online at http://www.imf.org/external/pubs/ft/wp/2003/wp03239.pdf.

96 World Bank, "Doing Business in 2005: Recent EU Entrants Are Top Reformers While Others in the Region Struggle to Reduce Red Tape for Business, Miss Large Growth Opportunities," Press release, 8 September, 2004. Available online at http://web.worldbank.org/WBSITE/EXTERNAL/NEWS/0,,contentMDK:20250836~pagePK:34370~piPK:34424~theSitePK:4607,00.html

97 UNDP, "On the Eve of EU Accession, A New UN Report Outlines How the Czech Republic, Hungary, Slovakia and Slovenia Can Achieve the Millennium Development Goals, Reduce Poverty and Curb Social Exclusion." Press release, 7 April 2004. Available online at http://mdgr.undp.sk.

98 "Chapter 1—A Brief Historical Overview," *Avoiding the Dependency Trap: Roma in Eastern and Central Europe*, Regional Report, UNDP Reports site. Available online at http://roma.undp.sk/reports.php?parent_id=1&id=191&scroll=191.

99 UNDP, "On the Eve of EU Accession."

100 "Chapter 2—Demography and Social Structures," *Avoiding the Dependency Trap: Roma in Eastern and Central Europe*, Regional Report, UNDP Reports site. Available online at http://roma.undp.sk/reports.php?parent_id=1&id=198&scroll=198.

101 World Bank, "Hot Topics," *The Roma in Europe and Central Asia* website. Available online at http://wbln0018.worldbank.org/ECA/ECSHD.nsf/ExtECADocByUnid/ED579276F12EEF75C1256E2E0059D79C?Opendocument.

102 Joanna Hyndle and Miryna Kutysz, "Russian Speakers in Latvia and Estonia," *CES Studies* 14 (August 2004): 96-100. Available online at http://www.osw.waw.pl/en/epub/eprace/14/PRACE_14.pdf.

103 World Bank, *The Millennium Development Goals in Europe and Central Asia*, 4.

104 Irena Grudzinska Gross, "When Pyramids Collapse: A Conversation with Fatos Lubonja," *East European Constitutional Review* 7.1(1998). Available online at http://www.law.nyu.edu/eecr/vol7num1/special/conversation.html.

105 European Commission/The World Bank, "What's the Economic Situation in the Region?"

106 Ibid.

107 European Commission/The World Bank, "What Is the Extent of Poverty in SEE?"

108 Ibid.

109 Ivan Szelényi, "Education, Ethnicity, and Single Motherhood: The Determinants of Poverty in Postcommunist Countries," *Transition* May–June (2002): 28–29.

110 IFAD, "Executive Summary: Dimensions of Rural Poverty", *Assessment of Rural Poverty: Central and Eastern Europe and the Newly Independent States*, 2002. Available online at http://www.ifad.org/poverty/region/pn/PN_e_1.pdf.

111 Parliamentary Assembly, *Recommendation 1588: Population Displacement in South-eastern Europe: Trends, Problems, Solutions*, 27 January 2003. Available online at http://assembly.coe.int/Main.asp?link=http://assembly.coe.int/documents/adoptedtext/ta03/erec1588.htm.

112 Norwegian Refugee Council, "Internal Displacement in Africa," *Global IDP Project*, January 2004. Available online at http://www.idpproject.org/regions/Europe_idps.htm.

113 World Bank Group, "Europe and Central Asia: An Overview."

114 Ibid.

115 World Bank, "Executive Summary," *Economies in Transition: An OED Evaluation of World Bank Assistance,* May 2004. Available online at http://siteresources.worldbank.org/ INTECA/Resources/transition_ economies.pdf.

116 World Bank, "The Developing Countries: Back on Track Toward Growth?" *Global Economic Prospects 2004* report. Available online at http://www.worldbank.org/prospects/ gep2004/full.pdf.

117 World Bank, "World Bank Report Highlights Need for Success at Cancun Trade Talks - Europe and Central Asia Growth Prospects Prove Resilient Yet Modest," Press release, 3 September 2003. Available online at http://web .worldbank.org/WBSITE/EXTERNAL/ NEWS/0,,contentMDK:20126054% 7EmenuPK:34466%7EpagePK:6400301 5%7EpiPK:64003012%7EtheSitePK: 4607,00.html.

118 See various "Poverty Assessments" for the specific countries at the World Bank's "Europe and Central Asia" page. Available online at http://web .worldbank.org/WBSITE/EXTERNAL/ TOPICS/EXTPOVERTY/EXTPA/0,, contentMDK:20204084~menuPK: 435735~pagePK:148956~piPK:216618 ~theSitePK:430367,00.html.

119 CIA, "Azerbaijan: Background," *The World Factbook,* 19 October 2004. Available online at http://www.cia.gov/ cia/publications/factbook/geos/aj.html (31October 2004).

120 World Bank, "Box 1.1. Consequences of the Civil War: Poverty Among the IDPs," *Georgia: Poverty Update* report, 10 January 2002. Available online at http://www-wds.worldbank.org/ servlet/WDSContentServer/WDSP/IB/ 2002/03/01/000094946_02021604020221/ Rendered/PDF/multi0page.pdf.

121 World Bank Group, "Europe and Central Asia: An Overview."

122 IMF/World Bank, "III. Policy Priorities to Reduce Poverty and Promote Growth," *Poverty Reduction, Growth and Debt Sustainability in Low-Income CIS Countries,* Joint IFI paper, 14 February 2002. Available online at http://lnweb18.worldbank.org/ECA/ eca.nsf/Attachments/PovertyReduction1/ $File/Joint+IFI+paper+growth&debt .pdf.

123 UNDP, "Overview," *Report on Democracy in Latin America: Towards a Citizens' Democracy,* 21 April 2004. Available online at http://www.undp.org/ democracy_report_latin_america/ exectve_summary.pdf.

124 United Nations Development Programme, "UNDP Launches Groundbreaking Report—"Democracy in Latin America: Towards a Citizens' Democracy," Press release, 21 April 2004. Available online at http://www.undp.org/dpa/pressrelease/ releases/2004/april/0421prodal.html.

125 Margaret Daly Hayes, "The U.S. and Latin America: A Lost Decade?" *Foreign Affairs,* 68.1 (1989). Available online at http://www.foreignaffairs.org/ 19890201faessay5941/margaret-daly- hayes/the-u-s-and-latin-america-a- lost-decade.html.

126 Ibid.

127 José M. Salazar-Xirinachs, "Economic Integration and Trade Negotiations in Latin America and the Caribbean at the Turn of the Century," in *Latin American Democracies in the New Global Economy,* ed. Ana Margheritis. Coral Gables: North-South Press at the University of Miami, 2003, p. 32.

128 Barbara Fraser and Paul Jeffrey, "Latin America Today: A Call for Economic Change," *National Catholic Reporter,* NCRonline.org, 4 June 2004. Available online at http://ncronline.org/NCR_ Online/archives2/2004b/060404/ 060404a.php.

129 Ibid.

130 Geri Smith, "Democracy on the Ropes; With Corruption and Economic Woes Rising, Latin America Is Disillusioned," *Business Week* 17 May 2004, 54.

131 UNDP, "Overview," 5.

132 Anonymous, "Contrary to Myth, Latin America Is Not Becoming More Unequal. Nor Is It Becoming Less So," *The Economist* 6 November 2003. Available online at http://www .economist.com/printedition/ displayStory.cfm?Story_ID=2193852.

133 Anonymous, "A Stubborn Curse," *The Economist*, 6 November 2003 <http://www.economist.com/ printedition/displayStory.cfm?Story_ ID=2193852>, (7 November 2004).

134 Juan Forero, "Latin America Graft and Poverty Trying Patience with Democracy," *The New York Times* 24 June 2004, A1.

135 President Alejandro Toledo, quoted in Forero, "Latin America Graft and Poverty Trying Patience with Democracy."

136 Anonymous.

137 Ibid.

138 "The Americas: Democracy's Low-Level Equilibrium; The Latinobarmetro Poll;" *The Economist* 14 August 2004, 41

139 *Meeting the Millennium Poverty Reduction Targets in Latin America and the Caribbean*, ECLAC, IPEA, UNDP report, December 2002. Available online at http://www.undp.org/ rblac/documents/poverty/mdg/MDGs- libro70.pdf.

140 Forero, "Latin America Graft and Poverty Trying Patience with Democracy."

141 Ibid.

142 Geri Smith, "Democracy on the Ropes."

143 Ibid.

144 United Nations Development Programme, press release.

145 Ibid.

146 The World Bank Group, "Doing Business in 2005: Latin American Nations Struggle to Reduce Red Tape for Business, Miss Large Growth Opportunities," Press release, 8 September 2004. Available online at http://web.worldbank.org/WBSITE/ EXTERNAL/NEWS/0,,contentMDK: 20250832~menuPK:34466~pagePK: 64003015~piPK:64003012~theSitePK: 4607,00.html.

147 Ibid.

148 United Nations Development Programme, press release.

149 Mark Malloch Brown, "Foreword," *Human Development Report 2002*, UNDP, 2002. Available online at http://hdr.undp.org/reports/global/ 2002/en/pdf/front.pdf.

150 UNDP, "Overview: Cultural Liberty in Today's Diverse World," *Human Development Report 2004*. Available online at http://hdr.undp.org/ reports/global/2004/pdf/hdr04_ overview.pdf.

151 The World Bank, "Development Projects for Indigenous Peoples," *Latin America and the Caribbean*. Available online at http://wbln0018.worldbank .org/LAC/LAC.nsf/ECADocByUnid/ 4D5BD6466372570185256D17005F3B 08?Opendocument.

152 Cesar P. Bouillon and Mayra Bovinic, "The Region's Poverty Profile: Who is Affected and Where?" *Inequality, Exclusion and Poverty in Latin America and the Caribbean: Implications for Development*, IADB. Available online at http://www.iadb.org/sds/doc/soc-IDB- SocialCohesion-E.pdf.

153 The World Bank, "Development Projects for Indigenous Peoples."

154 Amy Chua, *World on Fire: How Exporting Free Market Democracy Breeds Ethnic Hatred and Global Instability*. New York: Doubleday, 2003, p. 57.

155 Ibid., 69.

156 Ibid., 72

157 The World Bank Group, "What is the Informal Economy?" *The Informal Economy and Local Economic Development*, Urban Development site. Available online at http://www .worldbank.org/urban/led/informal_ economy.html.

158 World Bank, "Economy Characteristics," *Doing Business: Explore Economies*. Available online at http://rru.worldbank.org/DoingBusine ss/ExploreEconomies/EconomyCharac teristics.aspx?direction=desc&sort=5.

159 Andres Oppenheimer, "Hidden Economy's Strength a Mixed Blessing for Region," *The Miami Herald* 8 December 2002. Available online at http://www.miami.com/mld/miamiher ald/news/columnists/andres_oppenhei mer/4690696.htm?1c.

160 Barbara Fraser and Paul Jeffrey, "Persistent Unemployment."

161 Andres Oppenheimer, "Hidden Economy's Strength a Mixed Blessing for Region."

162 For example, see International Finance Corporation, *Extractive Industries Review* (available online at http://ifcln1.ifc.org/ifcext/eir.nsf/Conte nt/Home); S. Pegg, "Do World Bank Investments in Extractive Industries in Africa Contribute to Poverty Reduction?" (available online at http://www.eldis.org/static/DOC12729. htm); and World Bank, "World Bank Group Board Agrees Way Forward on Extractive Industries Review" press release (available online at http://web.worldbank.org/WBSITE/ EXTERNAL/NEWS/0,,contentMDK: 20237406~menuPK:34463~pagePK: 64003015~piPK:64003012~theSitePK: 4607,00.html).

163 Ricardo Ffrench-Davis quoted in Barbara Fraser and Paul Jeffrey, "Raw Materials Bring Few Benefits."

164 Summit of the Americas Information Network, "Education." Available online at http://www.summit-americas.org/ Quebec-Education/education-eng.htm.

165 "Education," *Advancing in the Americas: Progress and Challenges Summit Report2001-2003*, Summit of the Americas. Available online at http://www.summit-americas.org/ Publications/Advancing_in_The_ Americas/ENG_Education.pdf.

166 Suzanne Duryea and Carmen Pagés, "What Human Capital Policies Can and Cannot Do for Productivity and Poverty Reduction in Latin America," in *Latin American Democracies in the New Global Economy*, ed. Ana Margheritis. Coral Gables: North-South Center Press at University of Miami, 2003, p. 151.

167 Ibid, 101.

168 Anonymous, "Cramming Them in," *The Economist*, 9 May 2002. Available online at http://www.economist.com/ research/backgrounders/displaystory .cfm?story_id=1121601.

169 Suzanne Duryea and Carmen Pagés, "What Human Capital Policies Can and Cannot Do for Productivity and Poverty Reduction in Latin America," 156.

170 Ibid, 158.

171 Daniela Hecht, "Latin America: UN Focuses on Gender in Poverty Fight," The *Madison Times* 20-26 August 2004. Available online at http://www .madtimes.com/archives/aug2004_3/ glance.htm (10 November 2004).

172 Ibid.

173 Marcela Valente, "LATAM: Women's Rights Widen, but Poverty Persists," *Global Information Network*, 15 September 2004. Available online at http://proquest.umi.com/pqdweb?RQT =309&VInst=PROD&VName=PQD& VType=PQD&Fmt=3&did=000000693 221301&clientId=394.

174 Marcela Valente, "LATAM: Women's Rights Widen but Poverty Persist," *Global Information Network*, New York: September 15, 2004. Available online at www.globalinfo.org.

175 Ian Vásquez, "Economic Freedom and Confusion in Latin America," CATO Institute, 21 July 2004. Available online at http://www.cato.org/dailys/07-21-04-2.html.

176 Barbara Fraser and Paul Jeffrey, "Raw Materials Bring Few Benefits."

177 Tyler Bridges and Jane Bussey, "Economists Have Mostly Sunny Outlook for Latin American Nations," *The Miami Herald* 27 September 2004.

178 *Meeting the Millennium Poverty Reduction Targets in Latin America and the Caribbean*, 12.

179 *OECD in Figures: Statistics on the Member Countries*, OECD, Paris 2004. Available online at http://www1.oecd.org/publications/e-book/0104071E.PDF.

180 Stephen R. Shalom, "Poverty, Inequality, and Welfare," in *Which Side Are You On? An Introduction to Politics*. Boston: Longman, 2003, pp. 327–328. Available online at http://www.ablongman.com/partners_in_polisci/sampchps/SHAL%20cp12.pdf.

181 MSN Encarta Encyclopedia, "Poverty - VII: Measuring Poverty - A. International Measurements." Available online at http://encarta.msn.com/encyclopedia_761577020_3/Poverty.html#s110.

182 Shalom, "Poverty, Inequality, and Welfare," 328.

183 MSN Encarta Encyclopedia, "Poverty–VII: Measuring Poverty–A. International Measurements."

184 Tony Atkinson et al., *Social Indicators: The EU and Social Inclusion*. New York: Oxford University Press Inc., 2002, p. 5.

185 Michael Förster and Mark Pearson, *Income Distribution and Poverty in the OECD Area: Trends and Driving Forces*, OECD Economic Studies report, 2002. Available online at http://www.oecd.org/dataoecd/16/33/2968109.pdf.

186 Bernadette D. Proctor and Joseph Dalaker, *Poverty in the United States: 2002*, US Census Bureau, September 2003. Available online at http://www.census.gov/prod/2003pubs/p60-222.pdf.

187 LIS, "Introduction: Short Description–History—Where Are We Going?" Luxembourg Income Study website, 25 October 2004. Available online at http://www.lisproject.org/introduction/history.htm.

188 Johan Fritzell and Veli-Matti Ritakallio, *Societal and Changed Patterns of Poverty*, Working paper No. 393, Luxembourg Study Working Paper Series, September 2004. Available online at http://www.lisproject.org/publications/liswps/393.pdf.

189 John Micklewright, "Child Poverty in English-Speaking Countries," *Colloque: "Les Enfants Pauvres en France,"* 21 March 2003. Available online at http://www.cerc.gouv.fr/meetings/colloquemars2003/programme.html.

190 Ibid.

191 Ibid.

192 Joel D. Sherman et al., *Comparative Indicators of Education in the United States and Other G8 Countries: 2002*, NCES, May 2003. Available online at http://nces.ed.gov/pubs2003/2003026.pdf.

193 Ibid.

194 Jason O'Neale Roach, "One in Six Children Live in Relative Poverty," *British Medical Journal* 320 (2000): 1621. Available online at http://bmj.bmjjournals.com/cgi/content/full/320/7250/1626/i.

195 Pamala Wiepking and Ineke Maas, *Gender Differences in Poverty: A Cross-National Research*, Working paper No. 389, Luxembourg Study Working Paper Series, October 2004. Available online at http://www.lisproject.org/publications/liswps/389.pdf.

196 Ibid.

197 Karen Christopher, "Family-Friendly Europe," *The American Prospect* 13.7 (2002): 59.

198 Ibid.

199 John Iceland, *Poverty in America: A Handbook.* Berkeley: University of California Press, 2003, p. 78.

200 Peter Abrahamson, "Researching Poverty and Social Exclusion in Europe," *Journal of European Social Policy* 13.3(2003): 283.

201 Michael Förster and Mark Pearson, *Income Distribution and Poverty in the OECD Area: Trends and Driving Forces*, 19.

202 Ibid., 36.

203 Ibid., 24.

204 Bernadette D. Proctor and Joseph Dalaker, *Poverty in the United States: 2002*, 8.

205 MSN Encarta Encyclopedia, "VI: Poverty in Developed Countries–B. Other Developed Countries."

206 Johan Fritzell and Veli-Matti Ritakallio, *Societal and Changed Patterns of Poverty*, 19.

207 Michael Förster and Mark Pearson, *Income Distribution and Poverty in the OECD Area: Trends and Driving Forces*, 29.

208 *The Social Situation in the European Union: 2002, In Brief*, Eurostat and the European Commission, 2002. Available online at http://europa.eu.int/comm/employment_social/social_situation/docs/SSR2002_brief_en.pdf.

209 Bernadette D. Proctor and Joseph Dalaker, *Poverty in the United States: 2002*, 5.

210 Joseph Bruchac, "Indian Scenes from a Renaissance," *National Geographic* September 2004, 88.

211 Bernadette D. Proctor and Joseph Dalaker, *Poverty in the United States: 2002*, 7.

212 Adam Smith, *Wealth of Nations*, quoted in US Census Bureau, *Supplemental Measures of Material Well-Being: Expenditures, Consumption and Poverty, 1998 and 2001*, 3. Available online at http://www.census.gov/prod/2003pubs/p23-201.pdf.

213 Shalom, "Poverty, Inequality, and Welfare," 342.

214 Ibid.

215 "Finance and Economics: Why Welfare?" *The Economist*, Book review, 11 March 2004. Available online at http://www.economist.com/finance/displayStory.cfm?story_id=2498947.

216 Peter Abrahamson, "Researching Poverty and Social Exclusion in Europe," 282.

217 Bernadette D. Proctor and Joseph Dalaker, *Poverty in the United States: 2002*, 4.

218 "Finance and Economics: Why Welfare?"

219 Irwin Garfinkel, Lee Rainwater, and Timothy M. Smeeding, *Welfare State Expenditures and the Redistribution of Well-Being: Children, Elders and Others in Comparative Perspective*, Working paper No. 387, Luxembourg Study Working Paper Series, October 2004. Available online at http://www.lisproject.org/publications/liswps/387.pdf.

220 Ibid.

221 Johan Fritzell and Veli-Matti Ritakallio, *Societal and Changed Patterns of Poverty*, 22.

222 Dietrich Rueschemeyer and Miguel Glatzer, *Globalization and the Welfare State: A Research Summary*, The Watson Institute for International Studies. Available online at http://www.watsoninstitute.org/gfws/summary.cfm.

223 Jean Grugel, "Making a Statement or Finding a Role," in *Here to Help: NGOs Combating Poverty in Latin America*, ed. Robyn Eversole. Armonk and London: M. E. Sharpe, Inc., 2003, p. 33–34.

224 Ibid.

225 Ikubolajeh Logan, "Introduction," in *Globalization, the Third World State and Poverty-Alleviation in the Twenty-First Century*, ed. Ikubolajeh Logan. Burlington: Ashgate Publishing, Ltd., 2002, p. 6.

226 Ibid., 3–4.

227 Sebastian Mallaby, "NGOs: Fighting Poverty, Hurting the Poor, *Foreign Policy*, Sept/Oct 2004.

228 Ibid.

229 Ibid.

230 The World Bank Group, "Comprehensive Development Framework" website. Available online at http://web.worldbank.org/WBSITE/EXTERNAL/PROJECTS/STRATEGIES/CDF/0,,pagePK:60447~theSitePK:140576,00.html.

231 Ibid.

232 The World Bank Group, "Questions and Answers," PovertyNet website. Available online at http://web.worldbank.org/WBSITE/EXTERNAL/TOPICS/EXTPOVERTY/EXTPRS/0,,menuPK:384209~pagePK:162100~piPK:159310~theSitePK:384201,00.html.

233 Ibid.

234 The World Bank Group, Comprehensive Development Framework" website.

235 Gaby Ramia, "Global Social Policy, INGOs and Strategic Management: An Emerging Research Agenda," *Global Social Policy* 3.1 (2003): 80.

236 Pete Engardio et al., "Special Report: Global Poverty," *Business Week* 14 October 2002, 109–118.

237 Bureau for Policy and Program Coordination, "Overview," *U.S. Foreign Aid: Meeting the Challenges of the Twenty First Century*, U.S. Agency for International Development, January 2004. Available online at http://www.usaid.gov/policy/pdabz3221.pdf.

238 European Commission, *Annual Report 2004 on the European Community's Development Policy and External Assistance*, October 2004. Available online at http://www.europa.eu.int/comm/europeaid/reports/europeaid_ra2004_en.pdf.

239 Andrew Walker, "EU to Shake Up Development Aid," *BBB News*, 12 November 2002Available online at http://news.bbc.co.uk/1/hi/business/2492101.stm.

240 ADE, "Abstract," *Evaluation of Trade-Related Assistance by the EC in Third Countries*, EuropeAid, 24 May 2004. Available online at http://www.europa.eu.int/comm/europeaid/evaluation/evinfo/sector/951654_ev.htm.

241 UN, "What Is the Global Compact?" *The Global Compact* website. Available online at http://www.unglobalcompact.org/Portal/Default.asp.

242 RUGMARK Foundation India, "RUGMARK History." Available online at http://www.rugmarkindia.org/about/history.htm.

243 Pete Engardio et al., "Special Report: Global Poverty," 110–111.

244 Jessi Hempel, "Investing in the Greater Good," *Business Week*, Online Extra, 29 November 2004. Available online at

http://www.businessweek.com/magazi
ne/content/04_48/b3910419.htm.

245 Michelle Conlin, "A Talk with Oprah
Winfrey," *Business Week*, Online Extra,
29 November 2004. Available online at
http://www.businessweek.com/magazine/
content/04_48/b3910414.htm.

246 United Nations Foundation, "Our
Mission," *About Us*. Available online at
http://www.unfoundation.org/about
/index.asp.

CHAPTER 1

Anonymous. "Bakyt: Missing Out on School and Play Because of Poverty." Case Study. Childhood Poverty Research and Policy Centre. Available online at http://www.childhoodpoverty.org/index.php?action=casestudy&id=137.

Dawson, Thomas C. "Stiglitz, the IMF, and Globalization." *Transition* (May-June 2002): 12–13.

Development Assistance Committee. "Executive Summary." *In the Face of Poverty: Meeting the Global Challenge through Partnership.* DAC Guidelines on Poverty Reduction. OECD. (2001). Available online at http://www.oecd.org/dataoecd/18/19/1849018.pdf.

Engardio, Pete, et al. "Special Report: Global Poverty." *Business Week* (14 October 2002): 114–118.

G8 Summit. *Global Poverty Report 2001: A Globalized Market Opportunities and Risks for the Poor.* Genoa. July 2001. Available online at http://www.adb.org/Documents/Reports/Global_Poverty/2001/GPR2001.pdf.

International Development Research Center. "Take a Closer Look at Poverty." 10 January 2003. Available online at http://network.idrc.ca/ev.php?URL_ID=26048&URL_DO=DO_TOPIC&URL_SECTION=201&reload=1058151529.

Laderchi, Caterina Ruggeri, et al. "Does It Matter that We Don't Agree on the Definition of Poverty? A Comparison of Four Approaches." Oxford: International Development Center (2003). Available online at http://www2.qeh.ox.ac.uk/pdf/qehwp/qehwps107.pdf.

Naím, Moisés. "An Indigenous World." *Foreign Policy* 1 November 2003. Available online at http://www.foreignpolicy.com/story/files/story181.php.

OECD. "Poverty-Environment-Gender Linkages." Pre-print of the *DAC Journal* 2:4 (2001): IV-21. Available online at http://www.oecd.org/dataoecd/47/46/1960506.pdf.

Rekacewicz, Philippe. "Main Causes of Poverty in the World." Chart. Published in Global Environment Outlook 2000. London: Unep-Earthscan, 1999, 15. Available online at http://www.pover-tymap.net/mapsgraphics/index.cfm?data_id=12973&theme= poverty%20indicators.

Shah, Anup. "Structural Adjustments—A Major Cause of Poverty." *Global Issues.org.* 16 July 2003. Available online at http://www .globalissues.org/TradeRelated/SAP.asp#EarnMoreEatLess.

Stiglitz, Joseph. *Globalization and Its Discontents.* New York: W. W. Norton & Company, 2002.

United Nations. *United Nations Millennium Assembly Website.* Available online at http://www.un.org/millennium.

———. "United Nations Millennium Declaration." 8 September 2000. Available online at http://www.un.org/millennium/declaration/ ares552e.htm.

United Nations Development Programme Evaluation Office. *Monitoring Poverty. Essentials: Synthesis of Lessons Learned.* May 2003. Available online at http://www.undp.org/eo/documents/essentials/ MonitoringPoverty.pdf.

———. *Human Development Reports: Do You Know That.* Goal 1: Poverty and Hunger. Available online at http://hdr.undp.org/reports/global/ 2003/know_that.html#2.

———. Overview. *Human Development Report 2003.* Available online at http://hdr.undp.org/reports/global/2003/pdf/2003/hdr03_ overview.pdf.

U.S. Census Bureau. Highlights. *Global Population Profile: 2002.* Available online at http://www.census.gov/ipc/prod/wp02/wp-02001.pdf.

World Bank Group. *Millennium Development Goals: Malnutrition and Hunger.* Available online at http://www.developmentgoals.org/ Poverty.htm.

World Summit for Social Development. "Eradication of Poverty: Basis for Action and Objectives." *The Copenhagen Declaration and Programme of Action.* United Nations, 1995. Available online at http://www.visionoffice.com/socdev/wssdpa-2.htm.

Yergin, Daniel, and Joseph Stanislaw. *Commanding Heights*, Glossary. Available online at http://www.pbs.org/wgbh/commandingheights/shared/glossary/g.html.

Yergin, Daniel. "Threats to Globalisation in an Unstable World." *London Sunday Telegraph.* 9 March 2003. Available online at http://www.telegraph.co.uk/money/main.jhtml?xml=%2Fmoney%2F2003%2F03%2F09%2Fccglobl09.xml.

CHAPTER 2

Bunting, Ikaweba. "The Heart of Africa." *New Internationalist.* Special Supplement, January 1999. Available online at http://www.newint.org/issue309/anticol.htm.

Cohen, Daniel. *The Wealth of the World and the Poverty of Nations.* Translated by Jacqueline Lindenfeld. Cambridge and London: The MIT Press, 1998.

Cohen, Roberta. "Internal Displacement in Africa: Where Does the Responsibility Lie?" *Global Politics.* 26 May 2004. Available online at http://www.brookings.edu/fp/projects/idp/20040526rcohen.htm.

Edward, Miguel, and Mary Kay Gugerty. *Ethnic Diversity, Social Sanctions, and Public Goods in Kenya.* University of California. Berkeley: Department of Economics, 2004. Available online at http://emlab.berkeley.edu/users/emiguel/miguel_tribes.pdf .

Gary, Ian, and Terry Lynn Karl. "Executive Summary." *Bottom of the Barrel: Africa's Oil Boom and the Poor.* Catholic Relief Services. June 2003. Available online at http://www.catholicrelief.org/get_involved/advocacy/policy_and_strategic_issues/oil_report.cfm.

Lovejoy, Paul E. *Transformations in Slavery.* Cambridge University Press,

2000, derived from tables: 4.1, 3.4, and 7.4. Quoted in "Transatlantic Slave Trade: Origins of Slaves," *African History* section of the About online database. Available online at http://africanhistory.about.com/library/bl/bl-slavery-stats4.htm#table.

Norwegian Refugee Council. "Internal Displacement in Africa." *Global IDP Project.* January 2004. Available online at http://www.idpproject.org/regions/Africa_idps.htm.

Rosenberg, Matt. "The Colonization of the Continent by European Powers." *Berlin Conference of 1884-1885 to Divide Africa.* About online database. Available online at http://geography.about.com/cs/politicalgeog/a/berlinconferenc.htm.

Sachs, Jeffrey D., et al. "Ending Africa's Poverty Trap/Comments and Discussion." *Brookings Papers on Economic Activity* 1 (2004): 117.

Sachs, Jeffrey D. "A Rich Nation, a Poor Continent." *The New York Times* (9 July 2003): A21.

Saitoti, George. "Reflections on African Development." *Journal of Third World Studies* 20.2 (Fall 2003): 13.

ThinkQuest team 16645. *The Living Africa: About Our Site-Overview.* Thinkquest Library, 1998. Available online at http://library.thinkquest.org/16645/overview.shtml.

United Nations. "AIDS Orphans in Sub-Saharan Africa: A Looming Threat to Future Generations." *10 Stories the World Should Hear More About.* Available online at http://www.un.org/events/tenstories/story.asp?storyID=400.

———. "Excerpts from the Report: Combating HIV/AIDS, Malaria and Tuberculosis." *Economic Report on Africa 2003.* Available online at http://www.un.org/ecosocdev/geninfo/afrec/newrels/eraexcp.htm.

UNAIDS. "Regional Analysis." *Sub-Saharan Africa.* Available online at http://www.unaids.org/Unaids/EN/Geographical+area/By+Region/Sub-Saharan+Africa.asp.

United Nations Development Programme. "Overview: Cultural Liberty in Today's Diverse World." *Human Development Report 2004*. Available online at http://hdr.undp.org/reports/global/2004/pdf/hdr04_overview.pdf.

United Nations Population Fund. "Population and Poverty." *State of World Population 2004*. Available online at http://www.unfpa.org/swp/2004/english/ch2/index.htm.

———. "Selected Demographic Trends." *Sub-Saharan Africa: Demographic Indicators, 2004*. August 2004. Available online at http://www.unfpa.org/africa/demographic.htm.

Wooldridge, Mike. "UN Warns of Ethnic Diversity Timebomb." *BBC News* (15 July 2004). Available online at http://news.bbc.co.uk/1/hi/world/africa/3897479.stm.

World Bank Group. *Global Economic Prospects 2004 - Realizing the Development Promise of the Doha Agenda*. 2004 ed. "Appedix 1 - Regional Economic Prospects." Available online at http://www.worldbank.org/prospects/gep2004/appendix1.pdf.

CHAPTER 3

Asian Development Bank. "4.1. Recent Estimates and Trends in Poverty." *Key Indicators 2004: Poverty in Asia: Measurements, Estimates and Prospects*. Available online at http://adb.org/Documents/Books/Key_Indicators/2004/pdf/Special-Chapter-2004.pdf.

———. *Benefits of High Growth Must Reach Poor in South Asia, Says ADB Vice-President*. Press Release. 16 September 2004. Available online at http://adb.org/Documents/News/INRM/inrm200402.asp.

———. "*Poverty Remains a Major Challenge Despite Asia's High Growth*." Press Release. 26 Aug. 2004. Available online at http://adb.org/Documents/News/2004/nr2004093.asp.

———. *Working Together to Fight Poverty*, November 2003. Available online at http://adb.org/Documents/Events/2003/CAREC/Second_Ministerial_Conference/central_asia.pdf.

BIBLIOGRAPHY

Asian Human Rights Commission. *Exploitation: Child Illiteracy and Child Labour Are the Continent's Main Social Ills.* 29 September 2004. Available online at http://acr.hrschool.org/mainfile.php/0197/367/?Print=yes.

Associated Press. "North Korea Needs More Food, UN Says." *The Globe and Mail.com* (21 October 2004). Available online at http://www.theglobeandmail.com/servlet/story/RTGAM.20041021.wnkor1021/BNStory/International.

Chua, Amy. *World on Fire: How Exporting Free Market Democracy Breeds Ethnic Hatred and Global Instability.* New York: Doubleday, 2003.

Friedman, Thomas. Interview with Ray Suarez. *NewsHour with Jim Lehrer.* Transcript. 12 August 2002. Available online at http://www.pbs.org/newshour/bb/foreign_correspondence/july-dec02/tom_8-12.html.

IRIN News. "Central Asia: High Child Poverty Despite Economic Growth–UNICEF." *Reuters Foundation AlertNet* website. 14 Oct 2004. Available online at http://www.alertnet.org/thenews/newsdesk/IRIN/0c8db4337cc27a7900c6284f88ba0fe7.htm.

Khan, Sharier. *Poverty, Unemployment Stunts South Asia's Growth Graph.* OneWorld.com article. 1 April 2004. Available online at http://southasia.oneworld.net/article/view/82908/1/?PrintableVersion=enabled.

Lambert, Caroline. "At the Crossroads." *The Economist.* 24 July 2003. Available online at http://www.economist.com/surveys/PrinterFriendly.cfm?Story_ID=1922562.

Looney, Robert. Book Review of *Earnings Inequality, Unemployment and Poverty in the Middle East and North America. Journal of Third World Studies* 19.2 (2002): 319.

Pangestu, Mari. *"The Social Impact of Globalisation in Southeast Asia."* Working Paper #187. OECD Development Centre. December 2001. Available online at http://www.oecd.org/dataoecd/9/59/2731385.pdf.

Pomfret, Richard. *Central Asia since 1991: The Experience of the New Independent States.* OECD Development Centre. Working Paper No: 212. July 2003. Available online at http://www.oecd.org/ dataoecd/23/58/5961227.pdf.

"The Poor Arab Street." Global Agenda, Economist.com, 3 July 2002. Available online at http://www.economist.com/agenda/displaystory .cfm?story_id=1212573.

Rahman, Mostafizur. "South Asia in the Current Context." *OECD Policies Towards Development of Developing Countries: Learning from East Asia, Lessons for South Asia.* OECD Seminar. Paris. 10–11 June. Available online at http://www.oecd.org/dataoecd/36/58/31799439.pdf.

Wallace, Mike. "The Plight of North Korea." *60 Minutes.* 20 July 2003. Transcript. Available online at http://www.cbsnews.com/stories/ 2003/07/16/60minutes/main563623.shtml?CMP=ILC-SearchStories.

World Bank. *The Millennium Development Goals in Europe and Central Asia.* 2003. Available online at http://siteresources.worldbank.org/ INTECA/Publications/20219571/MDGs.pdf.

UNDP. "The Region Is Richer Than It Is Developed." *Arab Human Development Report 2002.* Press Kit. Available online at http://www.undp.org/rbas/ahdr/ahdr1/presskit1/PR1.pdf.

UNDP. "Executive Summary." *UNDP Releases the First Arab Human Development Report.* Press Kit. Available online at http://www.undp .org/rbas/ahdr/ahdr1/presskit1/PRExecSummary.pdf.

UNDP. *The Millennium Development Goals in Arab Countries - Towards 2015: Achievements and Aspirations.* 2003. Available online at http://www.undp.org/mdg/Arab_RegionalReport_english.pdf.

United Nations. "Extreme Poverty." *Millennium Development Goals: Report for the Kingdom of Saudi Arabia 2002.* Available online at http://www.undp.org/mdg/saudi.pdf.

Xinhua. "Chinese President Confident in Asia's Future." *China through a Lens.* 24 April 2004. Available online at http://www.china.org.cn/ english/2004/Apr/93899.htm.

Zagha, N. Roberto, and Oleksiy Shvets. *"Shanghai Conference: Scaling Up Poverty Reduction: Lessons and Challenges from China, Indonesia, Korea and Malaysia."* World Bank Group. Available online at http://lnweb18.worldbank.org/eap/eap.nsf/Attachments/Special +Focus+April+2004/$File/Focus+final+April04.pdf.

CHAPTER 4

Adam, Antonis, Theodora S. Kosma, and Jimmy McHugh. "Introduction." *Trade-Liberalization Strategies: What Could Southeastern Europe Learn from the CEFTA and BFTA?* IMF Working Paper. December 2003. Available online at http://www.imf.org/external/pubs/ft/wp/2003/ wp03239.pdf.

CIA. "Azerbaijan: Background." The *World Factbook.* 19 October 2004. Available online at http://www.cia.gov/cia/publications/factbook/ geos/aj.html.

European Commission/The World Bank. "What Is the Economic Situation in the Region?" *Economic Reconstruction and Development in South East Europe.* Available online at http://www.seerecon.org/ gen/econsitutation.htm.

Gross, Irena Grudzinska. "When Pyramids Collapse: A Conversation with Fatos Lubonja." *East European Constitutional Review* 7.1(1998). Available online at http://www.law.nyu.edu/eecr/vol7num1/ special/conversation.html.

Hyndle, Joanna and Miryna Kutysz. "Russian Speakers in Latvia and Estonia." *CES Studies* (August 2004): 96-100. Available online at http://www.osw.waw.pl/en/epub/eprace/14/PRACE_14.pdf.

IFAD. "Executive Summary: Dimensions of Rural Poverty." *Assessment of Rural Poverty: Central and Eastern Europe and the Newly Independent States.* 2002. Available online at http://www.ifad.org/poverty/region/pn/PN_e_1.pdf.

———. "Executive Summary: Regional Overview." *Assessment of Rural Poverty: Central and Eastern Europe and the Newly Independent States.*

2002. Available online at http://www.ifad.org/poverty/region/
pn/PN_e_1.pdf.

IMF/World Bank. "III. Policy Priorities to Reduce Poverty and
Promote Growth." *Poverty Reduction, Growth and Debt Sustainability
in Low-Income CIS Countries.* Joint IFI paper. 14 February 2002.
Available online at http://lnweb18.worldbank.org/ECA/eca.nsf/
Attachments/PovertyReduction1/$File/Joint+IFI+paper+growth
&debt.pdf.

Norwegian Refugee Council. "Internal Displacement in Africa."
Global IDP Project. January 2004. Available online at
http://www.idpproject.org/regions/Europe_idps.htm.

Parliamentary Assembly. *Recommendation 1588: Population Displacement
in South-eastern Europe: Trends, Problems, Solutions.* 27 January 2003.
Available online at http://assembly.coe.int/Main.asp?link=http://
assembly.coe.int/documents/adoptedtext/ta03/erec1588.htm.

Szelényi, Ivan. "Education, Ethnicity, and Single Motherhood: The
Determinants of Poverty in Postcommunist Countries." *Transition.*
May-June (2002): 28–29.

UNDP. *Avoiding the Dependency Trap: Roma in Eastern and Central
Europe*, Regional Report. Available online at http://roma.undp.sk/
reports.php?parent_id=1&id=191&scroll=191.

———. "On the Eve of EU Accession, A New UN Report Outlines How
the Czech Republic, Hungary, Slovakia and Slovenia Can Achieve the
Millennium Development Goals, Reduce Poverty and Curb Social
Exclusion." Press Release. 7 April 2004. Available online at
http://mdgr.undp.sk.

World Bank. "Box 1.1. Consequences of the Civil War: Poverty Among
the IDPs." *Georgia: Poverty Update.* 10 January 2002. Available online
at http://www-wds.worldbank.org/servlet/WDSContentServer/
WDSP/IB/2002/03/01/000094946_02021604020221/Rendered/
PDF/multi0page.pdf.

———. "Executive Summary," *Economies in Transition: An OED Evaluation of World Bank Assistance.* May 2004. Available online at http://siteresources.worldbank.org/INTECA/Resources/transition _economies.pdf.

———. "The Developing Countries: Back on Track Toward Growth?" *Global Economic Prospects 2004.* Available online at http://www .worldbank.org/prospects/gep2004/full.pdf.

———. "World Bank Report Highlights Need for Success at Cancun Trade Talks - Europe and Central Asia Growth Prospects Prove Resilient Yet Modest." Press Release. 3 September 2003. Available online at http://web.worldbank.org/WBSITE/EXTERNAL/ NEWS/0,,contentMDK:20126054%7EmenuPK:34466%7EpagePK: 64003015%7EpiPK:64003012%7EtheSitePK:4607,00.html.

———. "Hot Topics." *The Roma in Europe and Central Asia.* Available online at http://wbln0018.worldbank.org/ECA/ECSHD.nsf/ ExtECADocByUnid/ED579276F12EEF75C1256E2E0059D79C? Opendocument.

———. "Europe and Central Asia: An Overview." *The Millennium Development Goals in Europe and Central Asia.* 2003. Available online at http://siteresources.worldbank.org/INTECA/Publications/ 20219571/MDGs.pdf.

———. *Making Transition Work for Everyone: Poverty and Inequality in Europe and Central Asia* quoted in "Strategy, Implementation and Outcome," *Economies in Transition: an OED Evaluation of World Bank Assistance.* May 2004. Available online at http:// siteresources.worldbank.org/INTECA/Resources/transition _economies.pdf.

World Bank Group. "Europe and Central Asia." *DevNews Media Center.* Available online at http://web.worldbank.org/WBSITE/EXTERNAL/ NEWS/0,,contentMDK:20040935~menuPK:34480~pagePK:36694~ piPK:116742~theSitePK:4607,00.html.

CHAPTER 5

Anonymous. "Contrary to Myth, Latin America Is Not Becoming More Unequal. Nor Is It Becoming Less So." *The Economist.* 6 November 2003. Available online at http://www.economist.com/printedition/displayStory.cfm?Story_ID=2193852.

Anonymous. "Cramming Them in." *The Economist.* 9 May 2002. Available online at http://www.economist.com/research/backgrounders/displaystory.cfm?story_id=1121601.

Bouillon, Cesar P., and Mayra Bovinic. "The Region's Poverty Profile: Who is Affected and Where?" *Inequality, Exclusion and Poverty in Latin America and the Caribbean: Implications for Development.* Available online at http://www.iadb.org/sds/doc/soc-IDB-Social Cohesion-E.pdf.

Bridges, Tyler, and Jane Bussey. "Economists Have Mostly Sunny Outlook for Latin American Nations." *The Miami Herald* (27 September 2004).

Brown, Mark Malloch. "Foreword." *Human Development Report 2002.* UNDP. 2002. Available online at http://hdr.undp.org/reports/global/2002/en/pdf/front.pdf.

Duryea, Suzanne, and Carmen Pagés. "What Human Capital Policies Can and Cannot Do for Productivity and Poverty Reduction in Latin America." *Latin American Democracies in the New Global Economy,* ed. Ana Margheritis. Coral Gables: North-South Center Press at University of Miami, 2003.

"Education." *Advancing in the Americas: Progress and Challenges Summit Report 2001–2003.* Summit of the Americas. Available online at http://www.summit-americas.org/Publications/Advancing_in_The_Americas/ENG_Education.pdf.

Fraser, Barbara, and Paul Jeffrey. "Latin America Today: A Call for Economic Change." *National Catholic Reporter.* NCRonline.org. 4 June 2004. Available online at http://ncronline.org/NCR_Online/archives2/2004b/060404/060404a.php.

Forero, Juan. "Latin America Graft and Poverty Trying Patience with Democracy." *The New York Times* (24 June 2004): A1.

Hayes, Margaret Daly. "The U.S. and Latin America: A Lost Decade?" *Foreign Affairs.* 68.1 (1989). Available online at http://www .foreignaffairs.org/19890201faessay5941/margaret-daly-hayes/ the-u-s-and-latin-america-a-lost-decade.html.

Hecht, Daniela. "Latin America: UN Focuses on Gender in Poverty Fight." *The Madison Times* (20-26 August 2004). Available online at http://www.madtimes.com/archives/aug2004_3/glance.htm.

Meeting the Millennium Poverty Reduction Targets in Latin America and the Caribbean. ECLAC / IPEA / UNDP report. December 2002. Available online at http://www.undp.org/rblac/documents/poverty/ mdg/MDGs-libro70.pdf.

Oppenheimer, Andres. "Hidden Economy's Strength a Mixed Blessing for Region." *The Miami Herald.* (8 December 2002). Available online at http://www.miami.com/mld/miamiherald/news/columnists/ andres_oppenheimer/4690696.htm?1c.

Salazar-Xirinachs, José M.. "Economic Integration and Trade Negotiations in Latin America and the Caribbean at the Turn of the Century." In *Latin American Democracies in the New Global Economy,* ed. Ana Margheritis. Coral Gables: North-South Press at the University of Miami, 2003, p. 32.

Smith, Geri. "Democracy on the Ropes; With Corruption and Economic Woes Rising, Latin America Is Disillusioned." *Business Week* (17 May 2004): 54.

Summit of the Americas Information Network. "Education." Available online at http://www.summit-americas.org/Quebec-Education/ education-eng.htm.

"The Americas: Democracy's low-level equilibrium; The Latinobarmetro poll." *The Economist* 14 August 2004. 41.

UNDP. "Overview." *Report on Democracy in Latin America: Towards a*

Citizens' Democracy. 21 April 2004. Available online at http://www.undp.org/democracy_report_latin_america/ exectuve_summary.pdf.

———. "Overview: Cultural Liberty in Today's Diverse World." *Human Development Report 2004.* Available online at http://hdr.undp.org/reports/global/2004/pdf/hdr04_overview.pdf.

———. "UNDP Launches Groundbreaking Report—"Democracy in Latin America: Towards a Citizens' Democracy." Press Release. 21 April 2004. Available online at http://www.undp.org/dpa/ pressrelease/releases/2004/april/0421prodal.html.

Valente, Marcela. "LATAM: Women's Rights Widen, but Poverty Persists." *Global Information Network.* 15 September 2004. Available online at http://proquest.umi.com/pqdweb?RQT=309&VInst=PROD&VName= PQD&VType=PQD&Fmt=3&did=000000693221301&clientId=394.

Vásquez, Ian. "Economic Freedom and Confusion in Latin America." CATO Institute. 21 July 2004. Available online at http://www.cato.org/ dailys/07-21-04-2.html.

World Bank. "Development Projects for Indigenous Peoples." *Latin America and the Caribbean.* Available online at http://wbln0018 .worldbank.org/LAC/LAC.nsf/ECADocByUnid/4D5BD6466372570185 256D17005F3B08?Opendocument.

———. "Economy Characteristics." *Doing Business: Explore Economies.* Available online at http://rru.worldbank.org/DoingBusiness/ ExploreEconomies/EconomyCharacteristics.aspx?direction= desc&sort=5.

World Bank Group. "Doing Business in 2005: Latin American Nations Struggle to Reduce Red Tape for Business, Miss Large Growth Opportunities." Press Release. 8 September 2004. Available online at http://web.worldbank.org/WBSITE/EXTERNAL/NEWS/0,, contentMDK:20250832~menuPK:34466~pagePK:64003015~ piPK:64003012~theSitePK:4607,00.html.

———. "Mexico Makes Progress and Faces Challenges in Poverty Reduction Efforts." press release. 28 July 2004. Available online at http://web.worldbank.org/WBSITE/EXTERNAL/ NEWS/0,,contentMDK:20234053~isCURL:Y~menuPK: 34466~pagePK:64003015~piPK:64003012~print:Y~the-SitePK:4607,00.html.

———. "What is the Informal Economy?" *The Informal Economy and Local Economic Development*. Urban Development Site. Available online at http://www.worldbank.org/urban/led/informal _economy.html.

CHAPTER 6

Abrahamson, Peter. "Researching Poverty and Social Exclusion in Europe." *Journal of European Social Policy* 13.3(2003):283.

Atkinson, Tony, et al. *Social Indicators: The EU and Social Inclusion.* New York: Oxford University Press, 2002.

Bruchac, Joseph. "Indian Scenes from a Renaissance." *National Geographic* (September 2004): 88.

Christopher, Karen. "Family-Friendly Europe." *The American Prospect* 13.7 (2002): 59.

Eurostat. *The Social Situation in the European Union: 2002, In Brief.* European Commission. 2002. Available online at http://europa.eu.int/comm/employment_social/social_situation/ docs/SSR2002_brief_en.pdf.

"Finance and Economics: Why Welfare?" *The Economist*. Book Review. 11 March 2004. Available online at http://www.economist.com/ finance/displayStory.cfm?story_id=2498947.

Förster, Michael, and Mark Pearson. *Income Distribution and Poverty in the OECD Area: Trends and Driving Forces*. OECD Economic Studies report. 2002. Available online at http://www.oecd.org/dataoecd/ 16/33/2968109.pdf.

Fritzell, Johan, and Veli-Matti Ritakallio. *Societal and Changed Patterns of Poverty.* Working paper No. 393. Luxembourg Study Working Paper Series. September 2004. Available online at http://www.lisproject.org/publications/liswps/393.pdf.

Garfinkel, Irwin, Lee Rainwater, and Timothy M. Smeeding. *Welfare State Expenditures and the Redistribution of Well-Being: Children, Elders and Others in Comparative Perspective.* Working Paper No. 387. Luxembourg Study Working Paper Series. October 2004. Available online at http://www.lisproject.org/publications/liswps/387.pdf.

Iceland, John. *Poverty in America: a Handbook.* Berkeley: University of California Press, 2003.

LIS. "Introduction: Short Description–History - Where Are We Going?" Luxembourg Income Study website. 25 October 2004. Available online at http://www.lisproject.org/introduction/history.htm.

Micklewright, John. "Child Poverty in English-Speaking Countries." *Colloque: "Les Enfants Pauvres en France."* 21 March 2003. Available online at http://www.cerc.gouv.fr/meetings/colloquemars2003/programme.html.

OECD. *OECD in Figures: Statistics on the Member Countries.* 2004. Available online at http://www1.oecd.org/publications/e-book/0104071E.PDF.

Proctor, Bernadette D., and Joseph Dalaker. *Poverty in the United States: 2002.* U.S. Census Bureau. September 2003. Available online at http://www.census.gov/prod/2003pubs/p60-222.pdf.

Roach, Jason O'Neale. "One in Six Children Live in Relative Poverty." *British Medical Journal* 320 (2000): 1621. Available online at http://bmj.bmjjournals.com/cgi/content/full/320/7250/1626/i.

Rueschemeyer, Dietrich and Miguel Glatzer. *Globalization and the Welfare State: A Research Summary.* The Watson Institute for International Studies. Available online at http://www.watsoninstitute.org/gfws/summary.cfm.

Sherman, Joel D., et al. *Comparative Indicators of Education in the United States and Other G8 Countries: 2002.* NCES. May 2003. Available online at http://nces.ed.gov/pubs2003/2003026.pdf.

Shalom, Stephen R. "Chapter 12: Poverty, Inequality, and Welfare." *Which Side Are You On? An Introduction to Politics.* Boston: Longman, 2003, pp. 327-328. Available online at http://www.ablongman.com/partners_in_polisci/sampchps/SHAL%20cp12.pdf.

Smith, Adam. *Wealth of Nations.* Quoted in U.S. Census Bureau, *Supplemental Measures of Material Well-Being: Expenditures, Consumption and Poverty, 1998 and 2001.* Available online at http://www.census.gov/prod/2003pubs/p23-201.pdf.

Wiepking, Pamala, and Ineke Maas. *Gender Differences in Poverty: A Cross-National Research.* Working paper No. 389. Luxembourg Study Working Paper Series. October 2004. Available online at http://www.lisproject.org/publications/liswps/389.pdf.

CHAPTER 7

ADE. "Abstract." *Evaluation of Trade-Related Assistance by the EC in Third Countries.* EuropeAid. 24 May 2004. Available online at http://www.europa.eu.int/comm/europeaid/evaluation/evinfo/sector/951654_ev.htm.

Bureau for Policy and Program Coordination. "Overview." *U.S. Foreign Aid: Meeting the Challenges of the Twenty First Century.* U.S. Agency for International Development. January 2004. Available online at http://www.usaid.gov/policy/pdabz3221.pdf.

Conlin, Michelle. "A Talk with Oprah Winfrey." *Business Week* Online Extra (29 November 2004). Available online at http://www.businessweek.com/magazine/content/04_48/b3910414.htm.

European Commission. *Annual Report 2004 on the European Community's Development Policy and External Assistance.* October 2004. Available online at http://www.europa.eu.int/comm/europeaid/reports/europeaid_ra2004_en.pdf.

Grugel, Jean. "Making a Statement or Finding a Role." In *Here to Help: NGOs Combating Poverty in Latin America*, ed. Robyn Eversole. Armonk and London: M. E. Sharpe, Inc., 2003, pp. 33-34.

Hempel, Jessi. "Investing in the Greater Good." *Business Week* Online Extra (29 November 2004). Available online at http://www .businessweek.com/magazine/content/04_48/b3910419.htm.

Logan, Ikubolajeh. "Introduction." *Globalization, the Third World State and Poverty-Alleviation in the Twenty-First Century*, ed. Ikubolajeh Logan. Burlington: Ashgate Publishing, Ltd., 2002.

Mallaby, Sebastian. "NGOs: Fighting Poverty, Hurting the Poor. *Foreign Policy*. Sept/Oct 2004. Available online at www.foreignpolicy.com/story/cms.php?story_id=2672.

Ramia, Gaby. "Global Social Policy, INGOs and Strategic Management: An Emerging Research Agenda" *Global Social Policy* 3.1 (2003): 80.

RUGMARK Foundation India. "RUGMARK History." Available online at http://www.rugmarkindia.org/about/history.htm.

United Nations. "What Is the Global Compact?" *The Global Compact* website. Available online at http://www.unglobalcompact.org/ Portal/Default.asp.

United Nations Foundation. "Our Mission." *About Us.* Available online at http://www.unfoundation.org/about/index.asp.

Walker, Andrew. "EU to Shake Up Development Aid." *BBB News* (12 November 2002). Available online at http://news.bbc.co.uk/ 1/hi/business/2492101.stm.

World Bank Group. "Comprehensive Development Framework." Available online at http://web.worldbank.org/WBSITE/EXTERNAL/ PROJECTS/STRATEGIES/CDF/0,,pagePK:60447~theSitePK: 140576,00.html.

————. "Overview." Poverty Reduction Strategies website. Available online at http://web.worldbank.org/WBSITE/EXTERNAL/ TOPICS/EXTPOVERTY/EXTPRS/0,,menuPK:384209~pagePK: 162100~piPK:159310~theSitePK:384201,00.html.

————. "Questions and Answers." Poverty Reduction Strategies website. Available online at http://web.worldbank.org/WBSITE/EXTERNAL/ TOPICS/EXTPOVERTY/EXTPRS/0,,contentMDK:20175659~menuPK: 384209~pagePK:148956~piPK:216618~theSitePK:384201,00.html.

BOOKS

Chua, Amy. *World on Fire: How Exporting Free Market Democracy Breeds Ethnic Hatred and Global Instability.* New York: Doubleday, 2003.

Easterly, William. *The Elusive Quest for Growth: Economists' Adventures and Misadventures in the Tropics.* Cambridge and London: The MIT Press, 2002.

Friedman, Thomas. *The Lexus and the Olive Tree.* New York: Anchor Books, 2000.

Iceland, John. *Poverty in America: a Handbook.* Berkeley: University of California Press, 2003.

Landes, David S. *The Wealth and Poverty of Nations: Why Some Are So Rich and Some So Poor.* W.W. Norton & Company, 1999.

Stiglitz, Joseph. *Globalization and Its Discontents.* New York and London: W.W. Norton & Company, 2003.

Yergin, Daniel and Joseph Stanislaw. *The Commanding Heights: The Battle for the World Economy.* New York: Touchstone, 2002.

SELECTED WEBSITES

The Globalization Website
http://www.sociology.emory.edu/globalization/index.html

UN Millennium Development Goals
http://www.un.org/millenniumgoals

World Bank's PovertyNet
http://web.worldbank.org/WBSITE/EXTERNAL/TOPICS/EXTPOVERTY/0,,menuP K:336998~pagePK:149018~piPK:149093~theSitePK:336992,00.html

World Bank's Voices of the Poor Initiative
http://www1.worldbank.org/prem/poverty/voices/index.htm

OECD–Development Topic
http://www.oecd.org/topic/0,2686,en_2649_37413_1_1_1_1_37413,00.html

United Nations Cyberschool Bus: Poverty Curriculum
http://www.un.org/cyberschoolbus/poverty2000/index.asp

United Nations Cyberschool Bus–Poverty Briefing Paper
http://www.un.org/cyberschoolbus/briefing/poverty/index.htm

UNDP–Human Development Reports
http://hdr.undp.org/reports/view_reports.cfm?year=0&country=0&region=0&type=2&theme=13

PICTURE CREDITS

ABOUT THE CONTRIBUTORS

Nadejda Ballard is an international business consultant with clients in the United States and Europe. Nadejda also teaches international business and marketing at Rollins College in Winter Park, Florida. Originally from Bulgaria, Nadia holds an MBA degree with a concentration in International Business from the Crummer Graduate School of Business at Rollins College and speaks several languages. In addition to having lived and worked in Bulgaria, Switzerland, and the United States, Nadejda has traveled extensively to many parts of the world, including Assab, Eritrea, with a USAID food distribution operation, and rural China, on a research project. She has presented and published articles on cross-cultural communications, translation issues, and culture shock at the Society for Technical Communications, the University of Central Florida, Shanghai University of Science and Technology, and the International Academy of Business Disciplines, among others.

James Bacchus, is Chairman of the Global Trade Practice Group of the international law firm Greenburg Traurig, Professional Association. He is also a visiting professor of international law at Vanderbilt University Law School. He served previously as a special assistant to the United States Trade Representative; as a Member of the Congress of the United States, from Florida; and as a Member, for eight years, and Chairman, for two terms, of the Appellate Body of the World Trade Organization. His book, *Trade and Freedom*, was published by Cameron May in London in 2004, and is now in its third edition worldwide.

Ilan Alon, Ph.D., is Associate Professor of International Business at the Crummer Graduate School of Business of Rollins College. He holds a Ph.D. in International Business and Economics from Kent State University. He currently teaches courses on Business in the Global Environment and Emerging Markets: China in the business curriculum as well as International Trade and Economics in the economics curriculum.